UNDONE

UNDONE

A Grief Journey in Real Time

Joe Miller

XULON ELITE

Xulon Press Elite
555 Winderley Pl, Suite 225
Maitland, FL 32751
407.339.4217
www.xulonpress.com

© 2024 by Joe Miller

All rights reserved solely by the author. The author guarantees all contents are original and do not infringe upon the legal rights of any other person or work. No part of this book may be reproduced in any form without the permission of the author.

Due to the changing nature of the Internet, if there are any web addresses, links, or URLs included in this manuscript, these may have been altered and may no longer be accessible. The views and opinions shared in this book belong solely to the author and do not necessarily reflect those of the publisher. The publisher therefore disclaims responsibility for the views or opinions expressed within the work.

Some content taken from The Message by Eugene H. Peterson. Copyright ©2023.Used by permission of NavPress, represented by Tyndale House Publishers, a Division of Tyndale House Ministries. All rights reserved.

Paperback ISBN-13: 979-8-86850-742-7
Ebook ISBN-13: 979-8-86850-743-4

Dedication

"To live in hearts we leave behind is not to die."
—Thomas Campbell

This book is dedicated to the memory of my beautiful bride of forty-six years, Penny, who left me in body but will never leave my heart.

There were many dedicated and caring healthcare workers, including those special people from Journey Care Hospice, who provided care, concern, and love for her during the three months that she struggled with the disease. They made her life easier then, and I owe the world to them.

This book is also dedicated to those who have taken the grief journey brought on by the death of their loved one or to those who will ultimately take that journey. Each has or will grieve in their own unique way. May God be with you as you make that unwanted journey.

It cannot go unsaid what an enormous blessing our daughter Jennifer was during those difficult months, from the first diagnosis into the weeks following my bride's death. She came, unasked, from out of state on a one-way ticket to help care for both of us for many long months. She was

UNDONE

here for the duration, not knowing when it would end, leaving her family to do so. She came with her heart hanging out as she selflessly cared for her mother and me. Without her, I likely would have cracked. She was my anchor during that time. I can't thank her enough.

Joe Miller
#oldguywritesbooks

Death is inevitable for everyone. None of us will be denied passing on from this life. When it happens to a close loved one, life as you knew it comes undone.

~Joe Miller~

Table of Contents

Dedication. v

Epigraph vii

Introduction xiii

Preface xi

Part 1: The Shock. 1

   The Fluorescent Technicolor Elephant and Yo-Yo 3

   The Dark Side of the Elephant 6

   Uncomfortably Numb 9

   The Elephant is a Thief. No, he Robs. 12

   Abnormally Normal 14

   Wrestling with God in the Cranium Ballroom. 18

   Pissed at God. 20

Part 2: The Rough Part. 25

   Where's the off-and-on Switch?. 27

   Those Still Waters. 29

   Mirror, Mirror, on the Wall. 31

   A Great Thought for a Change 33

   Healing Moment. 35

   Tiptoed in the Room. 38

   I am NOT Going to Say Goodbye. 40

   A Veritable Flood 43

   And Just When I Thought. 46

   Embrace the Suck 49

Anguish is Real—Not Just a Word 51
Gonna be Okay 54
I'll Say Yes, Lord 56
It's Just Tough 58
Yes, it Sometimes Feels Like my Freaking Head is Exploding. . . . 60
One Last Dance. 63
The First Homecoming. 65
The Hardest Part. 66
The Lowest Point. 68
It's Not Goodbye 71
The Day That No One Wants. 72
We Rode the Horse Together 73
What Now? 75

Part 3: Moving On—Dance with the Limp 77
And Then What?. 79
Empty Space, Time, and Heart. 81
Memory Lane. 83
The Faucets That Are My Eyes 85
Just as She Would Have It. 87
A Different Kind of Visit. 89
Life Goes on, But. 91
I Wish, I Want 93
Teamwork. 95
Words Don't Sleep 97
A Penny for Your Thoughts. 99
A Bright Sunny Day, But. 101
Change 103
The Visit 106
It's a Matter of Form. 108

Perhaps the Worst First 111

Prologue. 113
About the Author. 118
Further Reading. 119
Resources. 121
Endnotes 124

Preface

Cruel. Cruel is likely the best way to describe what I observed and experienced happening in front of my eyes almost daily. I felt as if I was being robbed by the most cold-hearted thief, one who was taking my sanity from me. At times, I felt God was punishing me for all my past sins. I felt utterly helpless. And with that, I could find little hope, joy, or even peace.

It was June 20, 2023, in her doctor's office, when my wife and I heard what we never expected to hear. I remember the words well because those words began the most painful journey we had ever experienced. The words were, "You have stage 3 cancer in your lungs, and it has spread into the bone. We won't be able to get rid of it. All we are able to do is make you comfortable. It's very aggressive." Penny essentially received a death sentence, as did my heart. I felt empty from the shock.

In an instant, our lives changed forever, and so did the lives of our kids and their spouses, the grandkids, the great-grandchild, the extended family, and even those who had known and loved her over her eighty years. What had been normal flew out the window, only to quickly be replaced by new, different, strange, and what was to become abnormal.

Over three months, I watched what had once been a beautiful, vibrant, full-of-life woman wither away in front of my eyes. As I watched her fade, perhaps the only things that kept me going were her heart for others that never wavered and my need to care for her daily. She was the strong one on this new journey. I shared with her during one of our intimate conversations that we, together, were going to treat each day as if it was the best damn day of our lives with each other. Though I felt as if my legs had been chopped off from under me and that my heart had been ripped from me, my resolve was to make that happen. I found out how difficult that is to do because of how deeply grief can paralyze a person.

I had no idea when we first heard those horrible words come out of the doctor's mouth that the next three months and beyond could change lives the way ours did. I found out that's what grief and the grieving process do. There were good things that occurred during that time and bad things that happened. Many of them came as curveballs and from out of the blue. They all collided with my emotions in different ways, some with unpredictable results. That, again, is what grief does.

A grieving experience is a cruel experience.

Introduction

I'm going to get it out of the way right now. Grief sucks. Thus, grieving sucks.

~Joe Miller~

In *Undone*, I share my grief journey in real-time. It is raw at times but always honest. Many books and articles have been written about the grief process. In *Undone*, I invite you to walk with me in my personal grief journey from diagnosis until the death due to cancer of my beautiful bride. I also talk about life beyond the funeral and what it brings. The book is a deeply personal look into the mind of one living through the death of a close loved one.

In it, you can find insight into the grief process through a different lens. I discovered and experienced grief that came in three unique and definable stages. The first stage was from the initial period when she was diagnosed (when we had to face the elephant in the room squarely in the eyes) until I began to see the withering away of what a vibrant and beautiful woman she had been.

The second stage was bracketed from the time I accepted the premise that her death was imminent through the time she returned home under hospice care. During this stage, she struggled through radiation treatments and was ultimately hospitalized for nine days when her body could no longer fight the other complications. The stage ended when she finally returned home under hospice care.

The third stage was, and still is, the aftermath of her passing and all that it brought and still brings. This stage will never end. What was undone in the heart, soul, and psyche will never be healed. That's what grief does.

I had to lean into many other people to help me navigate this journey. It was a journey that I neither wanted nor prepared for. I think most folks would share that sentiment. No one wants to tread those waters, but we all must eventually. I discovered that there are neither guidelines nor rules that must be followed in the grieving process. This is because each affected person and their situation are different.

However, a common thread binds all who grieve or have grieved. That thread is called pain. In my case, it is a pain the likes of which I have never experienced. It hurts like hell. It's the pain that grips my heart with an iron fist, seldom letting go. It's a pain that numbs my mind as if it has been subjected to some horrible mind-altering drug. And it's a pain that squeezes my soul until it feels empty. Further, it comes in waves and with a randomness that often makes no sense. It comes at the most unexpected and unwanted times and can be brutal. It isn't pleasant. It seems lasting, which may diminish but will never completely disappear.

I hope this book lets you see yourself in the story. If that happens, then perhaps one of two things will happen:

1) You will be able to validate the feelings and reactions you experienced on a similar journey or
2) If you haven't experienced the death of a close loved one, you will be better prepared when the time comes to navigate that road.

I warn you that nothing in these pages has been sugar-coated or minimized. Feelings, emotions, and reactions don't play nice at times . . . at least mine haven't. Each of us in these difficult situations has been or will be sideswiped by surprises out of nowhere that will render our "normal" selves not so "normal." As I have had to learn, it's the nature of the beast.

Thank you.
Joe Miller

PART ONE
The Shock

> Love, not cancer, defines our last months together.
>
> By Sally Painter

In the first stage of my grief journey, I learned and came to appreciate much more thoroughly that real love is real, both as a receiver and as a giver. At first glance, that may not sound especially good. But what I found was that through embracing the imminent death of a loved one, one's perspectives of each other change profoundly. I genuinely believe that was the case with Penny and me. I also think that was part of God's plan for us. By the very nature of what was happening, despite the tremendously aggressive waves of emotions, nothing was more important than the moment we were experiencing at any given time. We lived in the moment, each moment. Those moments together can best be described as love moments that will last as warm memories forever in my heart.

Understand, though, there was nothing normal at that time. Everything felt upside down and inside out. The emotions I experienced then were unexpected, but as I learned, they were typical for the circumstances. That fact was a hard pill for me to swallow. According to my way of thinking, I was supposed to be the strongest person in these circumstances. At times, my strength had to come from my wife, who was facing the reality of her pending death better than I was. I was encouraged by trusted friends to "own" my emotions, to welcome them, and not to treat them as the enemy. I understood I would be in deep weeds if I didn't acknowledge and embrace them. Because of that, I was able to find strength at those times when it seemed impossible to do so. I believe that was what kept Penny so strong. God protects His children.

A Helpful Quote

"Tears shed for another person are not a sign of weakness. They are a sign of a pure heart."

Jose N. Harris[1]

The Fluorescent Technicolor Elephant and Yo-Yo

Does the above title sound at least a little bit weird? I hope so. Many people may understand once they know its meaning, but most will wish they never had to think about it.

Here's the skinny on the fluorescent technicolor elephant yo-yo. You have probably heard or used the term "the elephant in the room." Sometimes, it refers to that family member no one wants to talk about, the one everyone hopes doesn't show up next Thanksgiving. Or it might be a secret sin (whatever it is) that many of us struggle with. In that case, the elephant in the room would mirror the infamous thorn that Apostle Paul alluded to but never discussed. Here's

> We all have an elephant in the room, if not several. Many choose to ignore that it is there. Some are aware of it but decide never to talk about it.

the deal—we all have an elephant in the room, if not several. Many choose to ignore that it is there. Some are aware of it but decide never to talk about it. Occasionally, folks who have experienced life a bit will deal with it pragmatically and realistically. Sometimes, people talk very openly about it when that time in life comes, and the conversation can't be avoided. In this instance, I'm talking about death . . . something we will all eventually experience.

Nothing changes an ordinarily drab grey elephant into a technicolor fluorescent one faster than sitting in a doctor's office with a loved one (in this case, my wife of forty-six years) and hearing the dreaded and unexpected words "cancer" and "aggressive." The change in the color of our elephant from drab to stand-out bright was hastened because of the following words we heard: "third or fourth stage" and "we can't cure it; we can only manage it." Boom. The death sentences. The freight train is coming, and it can't be stopped.

So that's the elephant in the room part—the colored one. What about the yo-yo he has? Buckle up and strap in whenever an otherwise drab grey elephant turns into a technicolor fluorescent mess of an elephant. If you're anything like me, your emotions will mimic a yo-yo on drugs. Up and down, up and down, up and down, and all around. And it doesn't stop. And it won't. You are on for the ride whether you like it or not, whether you want it or not. Go ahead—try stopping it. Good luck, friend, and congratulations if you can. That's how I feel. That's what I am experiencing. And I can't do a damn thing about it. As I said, the train is coming.

I believe that my spiritual base is pretty darn rock solid. I believe in the sovereignty of God and His provision. I think His plan is perfect for me—whatever it is. And I trust that plan. He is God, and I am not. In these moments, none of that is enough to protect me when I get gobsmacked by a memory of us or a glimpse at her at just the right moment. In those instances, there is nothing that will calm my heart. I have heard that the calmness will come only from the second greatest healer behind God—time. I'll have to wait and see.

I don't see that elephant and his yo-yo leaving any time soon. Everything must run its course, and cancer is no exception. I'm sharing that elephant and yo-yo with a tight circle of close friends God has placed in my life. I'm pretty sure that they are strategic placements! Most of them will hand me a pair of sunglasses so that the brightness of the elephant's color isn't quite as bothersome. Some will walk beside me with their yo-yo, something I can learn from. All will love me, even though, at those times, I might be at my worst. And, because of this elephant, a new past begins.

The technicolor fluorescent elephant yo-yo is in the room, and he isn't going to go away.

The Dark Side of the Elephant

Something has prompted me to expand on what I shared in the last few pages. It's the title of an album I am particularly fond of, even though it's been fifty years since its release. I wish there were a way to insert one song from that album into these current pages as background music. It's called *The Dark Side of the Moon* by Pink Floyd. Take a brief break and turn it on so you can listen to it as you read.

The technicolor fluorescent elephant that I spoke of earlier brings a yo-yo. You'll no doubt hear about it occasionally in my writings. The yo-yo represents the wide range of emotions and feelings, their randomness, and their effect on me. I especially love the image of the elephant that I used because it speaks to the feelings I can't seem to control or have great difficulty controlling now. Let's look at those together. There are some green spots, but not many. They represent the few times I acknowledge to myself (own them) that I feel some emotions I don't want (or like). Accepting them allows me to experience them for what they are.

There are also a few white spots. Those represent the minimal periods in which my mind is still enough to find peace and calm. The blue spots represent the overall sense of gloom that doesn't want to disappear. There are a few more yellow spots, representing those times when I'm not overwhelmed but am edgy. I am impatient with others when I'm yellow, though I tend to be silent. However, if I am alone, I will voice that displeasure to myself and probably milk it for all it's worth. The orange spots are like a buffer zone between the emotions that I hold inside (trying to hide them) and the ones that I have a hard time controlling to the point that I will act out on them in a visible and sometimes hurtful way. The pink spots represent those times when I can't seem to help (or stop) an outburst while not caring at all whether someone hears it. That outburst ranges from sarcasm to inappropriate humor to words that should have never been spoken. The red spots represent when I feel a strong and sometimes visible sense of anger—at myself, the world, others, and sometimes God. The purple spots signify the continuing sadness I feel. And finally, there are the black spots. They represent those times when, and it's typically spontaneous or the result of some trigger, I feel despair and cannot control my feelings and will cry or wail. Those are the dark times, and purple and black are the dark sides of the elephant.

So, what about the dark side of the elephant? Each color holds space for a stage I might be going through. I can see the elephant in totality and see some good and some positive. I think about the rainbow and the covenant God made with us—that he'll never leave us. I get a glimpse of hope. I can get a peek at God's faithfulness and His purpose. Those times are not experienced very often.

For the most part, my focus is on the dark side of the elephant. It's there where the triggers are, the ones that drive an emotion or action. And I seldom see them coming. It's there where a well-meaning person will say, "I know exactly how you feel." Well, excuse me! I'm sorry, but no one knows exactly how I feel. I get angry when I hear that and must bite my tongue. I must remember that most folks are well-meaning, and sometimes people don't know what to say. I must give grace at those times, just like the multiple times I have been given grace.

When I'm alone and otherwise unoccupied, I'm generally on the dark side. Those times can bring crushing waves of emotions. Sometimes, someone will look at me with eyes that I know are telling me they are feeling my hurt. Again, crushing emotions are the norm at those moments. It's the dark side where emotions run rawest. It's the side where the most pain is felt. It's the side where it's not uncommon for me to feel a deep sense of hopelessness. The dark side is ugly.

In conclusion, the elephant who brings the yo-yo is indeed two-sided. There is a bright side. Even though it transparently shows the emotions as they are felt, it also shows hope and promise. The side brings God's faithfulness, despite circumstances, to the forefront. This side is the safe side—challenging but safe. The other side is dangerous, perhaps exacerbated by the fact that it is so easy to drift to it and feel compelled to stay there.

Uncomfortably Numb Yo-Yo

Another favorite song is also by Pink Floyd. It's a great one that's titled "Comfortably Numb."[2] It's been an earworm lately—I hum it, I listen to it, and it keeps playing in my head. That's what earworms do. I think it's happening because that's where I'm right now, except I'm not comfortably numb. I'm uncomfortably numb. And more so as the days pass. I'm feeling increasingly numb because of my emotions. They don't go away, and I can't stop them. What does feeling uncomfortably numb accomplish for me? It buys me time to squirrel hole the emotions away—categorize and shelf them in my head. I'm not sure that will work in the long-term. Still, for now, it's my way of preventing those spontaneous emotional outbursts, particularly the emotions that reduce me to uncontrollable crying or having to scream.

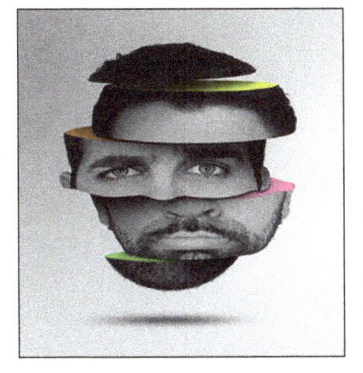

Sometimes—okay, more often than I care to admit—I feel like that guy. I feel like I'm not all together, and I'm probably not. But I pretend that I am. I don't want others to see the pain I'm feeling as I watch what is happening to Penny. I don't want others to see the anger that I feel inside—anger that stems from selfishness (which creates more anger piled on). This isn't how our journey was supposed to end. God has other plans (and I know that everything is by His plan), which, in turn, leads me to feel anger toward Him when I'm wrestling with Him over this interruption in our lives. I want to have a tantrum, a full-blown one at that, not just the sissy type of simply stomping my feet. No, I want the whole boat, and I don't care how ugly this eighty-year-old would look having one. But I don't do it because I want people to think

I'm doing fine with this adversity. So, I pigeonhole it instead. It's part of the yo-yo of emotions.

I also don't want others to know that I'm feeling a deep sadness that permeates my being. I don't want them to know about the fear I'm feeling as I look into a future that I can't see. Much of my life has revolved around uncharted waters, but this is different. Very different. Those other times, it was all about the challenge associated with the need to plow through those various waters. This is different. I don't see a challenge at all. For now, I see only the rough waters I am being thrown into that I don't want to go through. I can't swim in these waters. Another example is that I fear being alone. I've never been alone in my life. I fear what's going to happen to me. So even though it hasn't happened yet, I am feeling great loneliness and another type of fear.

Is it guilt that I'm feeling? I don't know. I find myself wishing it was me each day that passes. I feel helpless because I see what she is going through, and there is not a damn thing I can do about it to make her well. I can't make her better. I can't bring her back to the woman she once was. We've been told that she won't get well. Though we have never hidden from the topic of death, such as experiencing the deaths of family members, this is different. We have been gobsmacked by it. The elephant is in the room, and we can't miss him. He brought a range of emotions that he threw about like a crazy yo-yo.

I find myself experiencing shame. I feel a pervasive sense of shame over things past, instances when I could have been a better husband, father, and man. Shame for those times when I didn't consider her interests because I felt that my own were more important. Yes, I know all about grace and forgiveness, but that doesn't stop the shame from creeping in when I have too much time. And there's too much of that time because I don't care about doing anything to capture any focus I have left. Far too many "if onlys" are dangling in front of me, and I can't seem to ignore them.

The next logical step is for me to think about and talk about the things that trigger those feelings and emotions. I might do that. In the meantime, I'll keep switching between being comfortably numb and uncomfortably numb as I continue to be the elephant's yo-yo while I merrily (not!) keep pigeonholing my emotions.

The Elephant Is a Thief. No, It's a Robber!

I decided earlier that the elephant is a thief. Thieves are generally sly, stealthy, quiet, not very bold in a usually bold way (it's okay, I know what I mean), and typically unseen as they do their thing. They're sneaky. After some thought, I decided this elephant is far worse—it is a robber. It's bold, not sneaky at all, and indeed not quiet. It's obvious and very much in my face. I can see it doing its thing, which is robbing.

This morning, I was thinking about my day and what was in store because it's a holiday, and I would be homebound. I knew I had the job of paying close attention to my wife because our daughter, the caretaker, was gone for the weekend, taking some well-deserved time away. I had a laundry list of things to do—some of which were "must be done," some "should be done," some I wanted to do, some I didn't want to do, some I have never liked doing, and some I do like doing. That led me to the first reason I saw the elephant as a robber, not just a thief. There is nothing sneaky about it—he has robbed me of my "oomph." Yes, I'm old, but I'm used to having at least some "oomph." There isn't any left in the tank. I feel like the "oomph" is all gone. The tornado of emotions I have been experiencing has taken its toll on me.

The elephant has robbed me of desire and caring. I don't care how the house looks, and I have no desire to do anything about it because . . . drum roll . . . I don't have the "oomph." Honestly, I have also lost the desire and care to see friends. As horrible as it sounds, it's not that I don't care about them; it's just that it's too big of a "push" for me to reach out. I am withdrawing, and Lord knows I know that is not good.

I sense that the elephant has also robbed me of feeling. A look at the previous pages explains that. I'm feeling uncomfortably/comfortably numb.

Is there a better way to express this? I don't know. I only know what I think and what I don't feel. At center mass, there is emptiness.

I have been robbed of my sense of humor, laughter, and natural smile. Now, I feel I am forcing a smile, pretending there is something to smile about. There is nothing phony about that. It's safe to say that I have also been robbed of a couple of characteristics that I had to work hard at for years to learn and grow in patience and tolerance. If that is the case, both tanks are at a quarter full. How do I know? Because the buttons that can be pushed are hair triggers now. It no longer takes a hard, sustained poke at them to engage them. When they're pushed, I snap. Unfortunately, that snap is sometimes visible to others because I make little effort to control my reactions. Have I lost a sense of civility?

> I have been robbed of my sense of humor, laughter, and natural smile.

As bad as that is, I don't think I have been robbed of my faith in Abba Father. I still want to believe that He is in control, not me. He is God. I'm not. It's His purpose and outcomes that matter, not mine. And yet, I used the words "I don't think" a few sentences back because I feel that I may, in these moments, not feel as connected to and with Him as I have in recent times. As a result, I feel a sense of loss in that relationship. Has the elephant robbed me of complete trust and faith, as well as those other things it has robbed me of?

Abnormally Normal

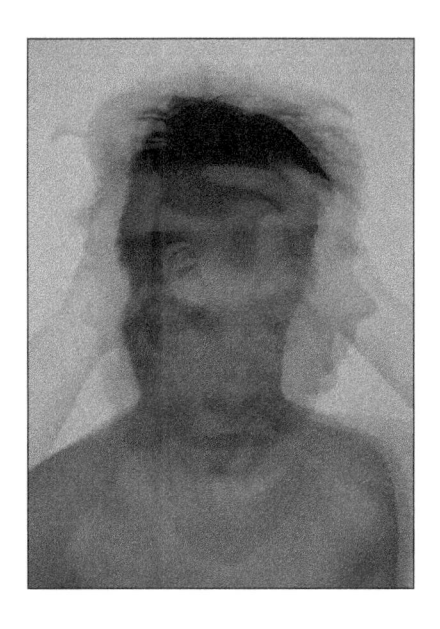

"What's normal, and what does it look like? Is there such a thing? Maybe it's the confusion of trying to sort those two questions out that's normal. Would that then be abnormally normal?"

~Joe Miller~

At first glance, the above image might justifiably cause you to think, "Oh-oh, this is going to be a dark read." If it hasn't already turned you off or away, read on . . . because it is anything but dark. The message it is wrapped around is surprisingly uplifting.

Have you wondered what others would see on a canvas where you drew or painted an image of yourself? What if it went deeper than that, and you had painted or drawn how you felt then? What would that look like?

I'm no artist, but if I were, I would have painted my recent feelings very similarly to what the above image speaks to me. In it, I see levels of fogginess (numbness), confusion, doubt, deep hidden anger, ferocious sadness, paralyzing loneliness, and fear. I have recently experienced all of them simultaneously in one place. It's the place I call the Cranium Ballroom. It's my head and the mind inside. That ballroom is *the* one place where I should never go alone. It's simply too dangerous, and I could find myself eaten alive there. It's happened.

I can almost hear you, having gotten this far in your reading. Are you saying, "Whoa, I thought you said this would be uplifting, and all I see is a deepening gloom?" My response to that statement would be, "It's coming."

I was uplifted during and because of being with a trusted friend over a long coffee huddle one afternoon. He is well-versed in this grieving thing. By the time we parted ways, I had had an epiphany. We got together initially because I *needed* to find out if I was at least a little "okay." I needed it because I felt utterly *not okay* because of the collision of emotions within me all at one time so much of the time. I honestly thought that I was losing it!

So, here's how those couple of hours went at a Starbucks with a man I knew that the Spirit had led me to reach out to. He leads the grief ministry at church. As soon as we sat down, that kind but piercing pair of eyes drilled into me. I knew this would not be a casual conversation, and I instinctively knew it was time for me to be honest and raw about what was happening inside me. Here's how part of that conversation went:

Don: "What's going on?" followed by dead silence, relaxed body language, and those eyes seeing into my soul.

Me: "I feel like crap, and I have been feeling that way. I can't not feel this way."

Don: "Why, what's going on?" So, I filled him in with the story about how cancer had invaded our lives (my wife and me) and turned it all upside down.

Don: "My wife died in similar circumstances nine years ago. We are all different, so I don't know how you feel, but I can imagine how you must feel."

Me: "I'm angry . . . in fact, I'm pissed off."

Don: "That's normal."

Me: "I feel a deep, deep sadness."

Don: "That's normal."

Everything I said was followed by his "that's normal." I shared about my fear, loneliness, hurting, unexpected outbursts of crying, anger at God, and confusion. And I kept hearing, "That's normal." Finally, I had had it . . . it was not normal, and I told him so rather unkindly. None of what I was experiencing was/is normal for me, and I got angry at him for even suggesting it. He smiled kindly, his eyes still piercing, and shared, "What you feel is normal. It may not be normal for you, but it is very normal for a person to experience all of what you have been feeling, given the upheaval in the lives of you and Penny. You're in an abnormal place now, experiencing normal emotions and feelings."

> **You're in an abnormal place now, experiencing normal emotions and feelings.**

So, there it was . . . the epiphany! I was abnormally normal, and I could be okay with that. He cautioned me that it would likely be this way for a long time. By accepting the abnormality of what is now a developing new normal in my life, I can learn to own and embrace anything I might be experiencing at any given moment during this journey and move on with it instead of trying to hide it, deny it, or pretend that it's not there. This was a great epiphany for me, courtesy of a friend. I pray I can keep accepting, owning, and embracing it. Abnormally normal—sheesh!

April 11, 2004

Does anyone know where I can find a copy of the rules of thought, feeling, and behavior in these circumstances? It seems like there should be a rule book somewhere that lays out everything exactly the way one should respond to a loss like this. I'd surely like to know if I'm doing it right. Am I whining enough or too much? Am I unseemly in my occasional moments of lightheartedness? At what date and I supposed to turn off the emotion and jump back on the treadmill of normalcy? Is there a specific number of days or decades that must pass before I can do something I enjoy without feeling I've betrayed my dearest love? And when, oh when, am I ever really going to believe this has happened? Next time you're in a bookstore, ask if there's a rule book.

11:54 p.m.

Jim ~Jim Beaver~ Life's That Way [3]

Wrestling with God in the Cranium Ballroom

Our journey is days shy of being four weeks old. That's the time since our world was turned upside down and inside out by the now constant presence of the technicolor fluorescent elephant and his yo-yo. Sometimes, it feels like that elephant has barricaded itself inside the Cranium Ballroom, aka my mind, and taken over. It can dictate what I think at any given moment and how I might respond in some situations. The truth of death, when it is up close and personal as it is now, is much different than when it is held at arm's length or beyond, which is where I always kept it. Because of that, it seems much easier for the elephant to keep the ballroom door open for unwanted guests. In my state of mind on this journey, I sense that the evil one is most likely to invite himself to the ballroom. There, he knows he can pull the most strings, push the right buttons, and try to garner the most attention from my already boggled mind (a prime weak spot for him to prey on).

There are many times now when I feel that the ballroom, once a pleasant place full of hope, promise, joy, calm, and peace, has been defiled. It's no longer a place where I can enjoy the pleasures of life's warm fuzzies. Instead, the Cranial Ballroom has become, for the most part, a place much less welcoming. It's become the one place I don't want to go to. One of the reasons is that once there, I usually find myself in a horrific wrestling match with God. Then I get super upset with myself for trying to wrestle Him. I know that I'll never win. I know that God will always prevail. I know that His plan and purpose matter. I know that He is God and that I am not. I know He loves me as a child of God more than I can ever know. And I know that His protective hand is just as it always has been, on me, protecting me. And yet, I wrestle with God. And I keep coming back for more.

I keep trying to find every little bit of solace during this part of my journey—some peace that somehow God is okay with my wrestling with Him. Even in my anger, loneliness, pain, sadness, emptiness, and fear, I have this sense that if I focused on anything other than those emotions, I might—no, I will—hear that sweet voice telling me, "It's okay, *little buddy, I got this, and I have you. Thanks for bringing your stuff to the ballroom so we can wrestle with it. You see, you're not wrestling with me . . . you're wrestling with the evil one, and I got your back because I know you are having weak moments because of all this.*"

I need to focus less on the actual emotions and more on what I want and need to hear from Him. Perhaps the best way to achieve that will be to shower between wrestling matches and keep on keeping on.

> "It's okay, little buddy, I got this, and I have you. Thanks for bringing your stuff to the ballroom so we can wrestle with it. You see, you're not wrestling with me . . . you're wrestling with the evil one, and I got your back because I know you are having weak moments because of all this."

Pissed at God

There. I said it. I said out loud what I was afraid to say. I was worried because I thought I would be judged. Afraid because no one is supposed to say something like that. Especially me. I'm that guy who so many feel has it all together, that guy who is a rock-solid Christian, that man who "we look up to." And the thought didn't escape me that a lightning bolt would instantly rip out of the sky and incinerate me on the spot. That goes back to my childhood days of learning the Ten Commandments. As a young lad, I took those "Thou shalt nots" further. My mind went to "But what if I do?" Then I could see the big foot coming out of the sky to squash me like a bug. Maybe it's fear of losing the respect that others have for me. Perhaps it's fear that surely God will not like it one iota, and then, who knows what will happen. My imagination has no limits on that one.

So, what prompted this unusual discussion? The world as I know it has been turned upside down. I feel as though my heart has been ripped out. I am hurting. I am deeply saddened. Most days, I can't "get it together." I'm tired of leaning into that "God has a plan" thing and that "God's got this" thing. And sometimes it's that simple thing that I should feel gratitude for—"I'm here for you." The biggest thing about this is what's been happening inside me. It's the one thing that I couldn't bring myself to admit—that I'm pissed at God. Yet today, I feel good about it. I am feeling less tension and inner stress, and today, I have felt a sense of calm that I haven't felt since I first heard of my wife's cancer. Why is that?

Yesterday was, for lack of a better term and to be clear, "a bitch." Perhaps you have experienced one of those kinds of days. My emotions were raw, and I had a level of anger laying just under the surface that was ominous as well as dangerous. Out of the blue, a dear brother reached out as if he could sense that things were not good with me. He was spot on—things weren't good. Surprisingly, I didn't want to retreat or back away or hide. I wanted to be with him, so we decided to get together for a late afternoon meal. I wanted to be with him because I knew I needed to. He can read me like a book, and the rawness doesn't faze him. He accepts me as I am and always has.

I love it when someone cuts to the chase and doesn't beat around the bush, especially when their steady, non-readable eyes stare into mine while waiting for my answer to a direct, pointed question. Yep, no bush-beating at all. When those infrequent moments occur, my transparency level seems to max out. I can't not be raw and honest in those moments. So, when those eyes were homing in on whatever they were seeing inside my head (I'm pretty sure they were seeing more than this ugly face!), I had to tell the ugly truth—that I was angry at God and felt guilt, shame, and confusion because of it. After all, I'm not supposed to get angry with God. Thus, I wrote about the wrestling match previously.

Then, the most fabulous thing since sliced cheese came about. My wise, well-versed friend asked me why not—why couldn't or shouldn't I get angry with God? But before I go into more detail, let me share a bit of a backstory first. It dawned on me then, and particularly more so today, the day after that discussion, that I was withdrawing from God—I wasn't (or haven't been) in the Word except for desperation/foxhole times over this past month, and my prayer life has sucked as well. Why is that when I know better? Because I had accepted the "lie" that somehow it was inappropriate to be pissed at God, and my embarrassment stood in the way of my doing what I should do.

My friend brought to light a few characters from the Bible who were angry at God, and he talked about some of them: Abraham, Moses, David, Jonah, and I think we are all aware of Big Mouth Peter! So, there I was, all kinked up about "my" problems and completely missing the point that our all-knowing God knows all that is going on in our lives—even mine. And I was missing the fact that He does want to "talk things over," and His MO is through the prayer that He invites me to have with Him. He's been waiting for that conversation because He already knows the issues. He wants my two cents' worth—even if it includes telling Him how angry I am with Him. For instance, we all know that David put Goliath down. Recently, I've been feeling that my Goliath has just stomped the crap out of me. Mary and Martha got their miracle when Lazarus returned from the dead. My mind wondered, "Where in the hell is my miracle?" With that kind of thinking, it's no wonder that I've been pissed at God. Who wouldn't be? Jeremiah came to a hair width from cursing God out. I've come a hair's width from not cursing God out.

Miller, the great encourager (evidently for everyone else but himself), had paid no attention to some of his own advice, advice he has shared frequently with others: 1) God will never give us more than we can take; 2) God does know what's going on. There are no secrets, so include Him in the process; 3) truly great lessons and revelations come out of pain and trying times—and not out of successes and pleasant times; and 4) God is never not walking right alongside us. He will not abandon His children.

I don't want to be a Debbie Downer because that dress fits me like crap. Besides, it doesn't look good on me. So, here's what I think I will try. I will try to remember Abraham, Moses, David, Jonah, Peter, and all those others who expressed their displeasure about their life circumstances to God. And I must remember that none of them fried because a lightning bolt suddenly hit them. None of them were cut off from God by God. None of them were punished for being truthful and open about themselves as they "talked" to God. Hey, for all I know, they may have even yelled—like I have wanted to. So, I started the day out this morning by just telling God that I was pissed at Him and that we had a couple of things to go over (meaning, mostly stuff about me). And we talked for a while and several times during the day. And, you know what? Today, my emotions haven't been nearly as raw as they have been recently. I smiled a time or two today. I certainly have felt "freer" inside. And I've been okay with myself for being pissed at God in the first place. Another friend, I am sure, would say, "That's normal."

I guess I have some reading to catch up on and some further conversations. He'll be waiting. He's always home. And He doesn't care that I'm pissed. Gotta love a guy like that!

PART 2
The Rough Part

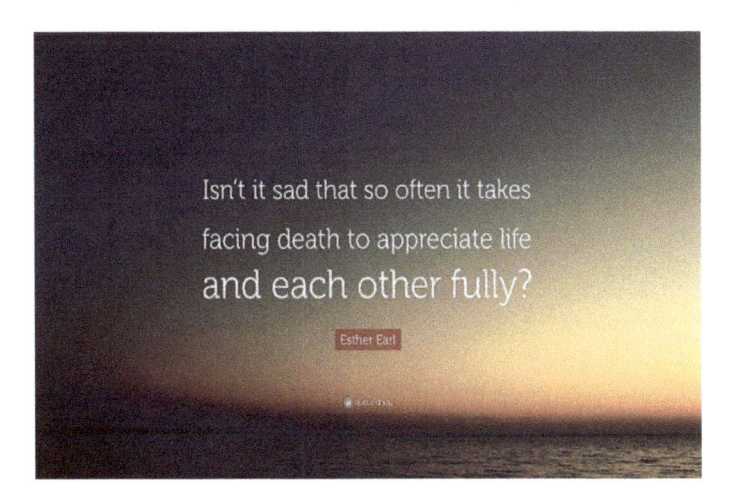

> Isn't it sad that so often it takes facing death to appreciate life **and each other fully?**
>
> — Esther Earl

There came a point in my grief journey when I sensed a shift in what was going on inside me. In what I call the second stage of my grief journey, the emotional upheaval I was experiencing subtly changed. The pain in my heart didn't leave or diminish. It grew, but it was different. By then, we had done all our business. We both forgave each other for those things that we felt the need to express during those deeply personal times we shared, and our total focus automatically turned toward a full appreciation of what our forty-six years together meant to each of us. We both acknowledged the coming end of our lives together. While the pain seemed more significant, its sting was shrouded

> Our hearts were paired in the now, and that gave each of us pause to embrace, in a new light, the pain of ultimately parting instead of dreading it.

with a deep sense of gratitude for each other and for the time we had had. There were no more bygones to be bygones. Our hearts were paired in the now, and that gave each of us pause to embrace, in a new light, the pain of ultimately parting instead of dreading it.

I came to love her more deeply than I ever thought possible. We both knew that we would not be saying goodbye. We would be saying, "See you later," in our hearts with a sense of joyous anticipation.

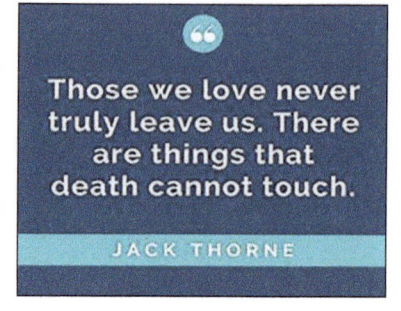

> Those we love never truly leave us. There are things that death cannot touch.
>
> JACK THORNE

Where's the Off-and-On Switch?

I remember times when I joked about the "thought police." I also clearly remember times when I was still on social media and declared myself (in my head) chief of the thought police on many occasions. I quit that job because the pay wasn't high enough, and in time, I found that I couldn't stand myself getting embroiled in things that didn't concern me.

Nowadays, I'm not looking for the thought police. Instead, I'm looking for, wishing for, the thought switch. I've learned that the longer this journey goes on, the more range my thoughts cover. They run the gamut from highs to lows and back to highs, from crazy to insane, from calm to wild, from loud to quiet, from silent to out loud, from one emotion to another—one right after the other, and from subtle to shocking (as in, "where the hell did that come from"). I wish there were "that" switch to turn off my thinker when it goes haywire like that. Sometimes, it needs to stop pumping out some of those thoughts about this whole journey that get me going. As I watch the love of my life withering away from cancer, from being "fine" one moment and in excruciating pain the next, from being lucid to being out of it from the pain meds, my thought machine goes into overdrive. That results in me being a hot mess train wreck.

For example, a "revelation" hit me while driving to work this morning. It was one I didn't anticipate or had considered before. The friend who keeps telling me that so much of what I am experiencing is normal would likely tell me, "That's normal," if I shared the revelation with him. Who knows, maybe it is. But it doesn't change that my revelation was far from enjoyable. The crazy thing is that I was in an excellent trigger-free frame of mind (I was happy, for a change) when the thought snuck in unannounced.

The "revelation" was, "This seriously looks like I'm going to be a widower . . . what will I do? What's going to happen?"

It's incredible how such a thought can throw a wet blanket all over an otherwise good day. That's because it immediately, uninvited, took on squatting rights in the Cranium Ballroom, which is my head. Frankly, out of that thought came many other related thoughts, each of which, like the "revelation" itself, were/are just conjecture. I'm not God, and I certainly don't know what will happen or when, but the squatter in the Ballroom didn't pay any attention to that.

Where is the off-and-on switch to my mind so that these wild thoughts can be stopped? That said, I know there isn't one because of what I experienced today, which I will experience again and again. It's a normal part of the grieving process. There's that word again.

> *"The key is in accepting your thoughts, all of them, even the bad ones. Accept thoughts, but don't become them. Understand, for instance, that having a sad thought, even having a continual succession of sad thoughts, is not the same as being a sad person. You can walk through a storm and feel the wind but you know you are not the wind."*
>
> ~Matt Haig~[4]

Those Still Waters

I'm neither a historian nor a researcher—I'm not wired that way. But I do have an imagination, and I like to use it. In my mind, I can see these as the green pastures and the still waters that David wrote about. Yes, it's from that wonderfully soothing and always on-time 23rd Psalm.

> "The Eternal is my shepherd; He cares for me always. He provides me rest in rich, green fields beside streams of refreshing water. He soothes my fears; He makes me whole again, steering me off worn, hard paths to roads where truth and righteousness echo His name"
> (Ps. 23:1–3 MSG).

Many days are comprised of anything but the calmness of still waters or streams of refreshing water I crave. I don't feel as if my fears are being soothed. And the rocks that I trip over are anything but gentle roads. I even wonder at times—does He care about me? My thoughts go to what I wouldn't give for the kind of rest (in my heart) that the shepherd's sheep find in the rich green fields beside those streams.

It should be no surprise that I sometimes feel that way. I think anyone in my circumstances (other than one with a stone-cold heart) would feel the same way. So, I'll go again to that place that I dig into—that I'm just human, and what I'm experiencing is, unfortunately, "normal." So, what am I to do? I'll continue to try to lean into the 23rd Psalm—something I've done before when I have felt that I've been beaten up, beaten down, or trashed and abandoned.

I found a YouTube video a while back. It's called Psalm 23-The Voice[5], created and posted by Thomas Nelson Publishers. Re-reading the psalm in several different versions, listening to this, and pondering about myself and where I am presently has given me a glimpse of hope. As I see the one closest to me withering away right before my eyes, hope is hard to grasp and hold on to, let alone find, so I'm glad for those glimpses. Ah, for the still waters.

Mirror, Mirror on the Wall

I imagine everyone in the country looks into a mirror at least once daily. We guys do it when we brush our teeth, wash our faces, or gaze at the handsome self our minds declare us to be. Women? Well, they must fluff their hair and do the makeup, right? And teens? Just the words "socially acceptable" say it all because in the minds of so many, the ideas of beauty and stud-ness translate to social acceptability.

These days, I'm not too fond of the mirror. Why? Because when I glance at it, it reminds me of me—oh, wait, it *is* me! I should have said that it reminds me of what I have become. It's scary when I look at it because if I think about it, I realize that that is exactly what others see. What is that mirror showing?

It's not the wrinkles that bother me. They were hard and honorably earned. I wear them like a badge of honor. To some, they may indicate wisdom buried under the skin. It's not the ruddiness of the face—again, well-earned and now honored. To some, that may indicate a life experience that could hold some value for a questioning mind or even one seeking wisdom. No, what I see reflected during this period is a frown that feels like it has been welded to my face. Along with the frown, I see an almost perpetual scowl, one of such a magnitude that it clears the path for headaches. I see the valleys where the tears flow downward to drip off the chin. I see the slits of once wide-open eyes that seem to hold nothing but sadness. There's no life in them. I see a stubborn chin that struggles and quivers to control emotions. I see pain in that face that brings a hollowness to the eyes that already reflect sadness.

Yes, I'm not too fond of the mirror because I can't see myself. I see a new me that I'm told is "normal." And when I see that new me, I can see the tears start to roll down those valleys. It's hard to hold them back. Some of those tears are from looking at something different in the mirror and my anger at myself for being unable to do anything about the new differences. And I know that is precisely what others are seeing, and it makes them uncomfortable because it places them in the awkward position of not knowing what to say or do.

I repeatedly tell myself that God doesn't see the Joe in the mirror that I am seeing. He's not seeing the countenance on Joe that others are seeing. God is seeing *all* the pain and sadness, the struggling and the uncertainties, and He's hearing the questions. He's also hearing and seeing one of His children who He deeply cares for, loves, and never has or will let down. He's seeing His creation, and He sees no surprises. That's all that the guy in the mirror can latch onto at times, and when he does, he finds comfort in it . . . if only for a fleeting time.

That leaves but one question: Why don't I try to look differently at the guy in the mirror more often? Mirror, mirror on the wall, why are you so agonizingly truthful?

A Great Thought for a Change . . .

Dang! That God of ours . . . He's pretty darn smart. He is. I've heard, read, and often spoken of His propensity to use broken, wounded people like me for glorious purposes. I've seen it in action in this world that we live in. And it's always beautiful to see the outcomes of His plans. Those engineered by me, well, they never seem to turn out quite as well as His.

If you have read this book up to this point, you probably have sensed that this old curmudgeon has been sitting on the pity pot for a few months. Some in my circle (okay, probably all) who know the circumstances beyond what I have written about would probably say, "That's normal." That term seems to be my best verbal pal these days.

Those who know me well also know of a years-long struggle I have experienced within my heart and in the Cranium Ballroom, the dance floor for the demons in my mind. That struggle has been knowing that my wife and I are unevenly yoked. I am a believer. She has shown no indication of a personal relationship with Jesus. She has always been one of those "well, I'm a good person" people. An apparent relationship with Jesus was absent in her life. This has been a concern to me for years. I have always sensed that any forays into the subject with her have fallen into dead-air space. It's been disheartening. I've been sad about it. I would often get frustrated by it. Over time, I have found myself grieving that fact more and more.

So, here we are now. She's aware of her stage 3 aggressive lung cancer. My frustration and anxiety have ramped up because I have been hoping and praying that she won't become a dearly departed one without having a foundation centered on Jesus. Well, low and behold, He took care of that little detail. He put the right words in my mouth courtesy of a dear friend. And Penny accepted and acknowledged the presence of Jesus in her life and what He did for her. She has fully welcomed prayer with her beyond the occasional grace before meals when the family is gathered or at funerals, weddings, or baptisms. Prayer, to her, has moved from an obligation to a conversation from the heart. Yes, we've been praying together, holding hands on her sick bed, praying. And it's been great. I can't begin to express how much that has changed our relationship in such a very short time.

This has been a ginormous deal. I've spent the past couple of months struggling with the terrible doldrums. Smiles (the real ones, not the fake ones) have been few and far between. Who would want to smile when watching a spouse with no apparent relationship with Jesus wither away? So yes, the whole scenario about her acceptance and praying *is* ginormous to me because of what happened last night. My prayer with her was different last night before we turned in. Different in a good way. I don't know what it was, but it felt so different. And then, as I was getting ready to shut down for the day a bit later, the light bulb came on . . . in a huge way.

It dawned on me that God's plan *is* at work and that He *is* seeing it through. He is using this time of all these " normal" things and moments to work His plan because it is His plan. Could it be that this nasty illness has been the tool to bring about the change in her heart and mine as well? I'll say it. When the light bulb in the ballroom went on last night, when that eureka moment occurred, I accepted that God is not only using me for His noble purpose but also this illness and the changes it has brought to what was once a normal life. I don't know why I didn't see that before. Perhaps I was just too wrapped up in all that "normal" stuff, such as sadness, grief, anger, yada, yada. But He certainly took care of that.

Dang, that God of ours is smart.

Healing Moment

How many times do you suppose the words "Can anything else possibly happen?" have crossed the mind of a caregiver for a terminally ill loved one? From increasing levels of pain to losing the desire to eat and drink to falling out of bed and incurring an injury to pooping in the bed, it shouldn't surprise anyone that it would happen, especially to those caregivers with no prior experience. To use a term that I have a love/hate relationship with—it's normal.

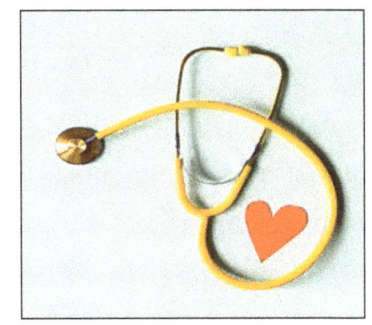

When one is watching a loved one slowly fade away daily from a lingering and progressive illness, it's the unknowns that feed that thought. What's going to happen next, one thinks. When is the next surprise going to pop up? How bad will the following incident be? Will I be able to handle it and know what to do? Those unknowns are depressing and work negatively on our human systems—our spirituality, emotions, and physical condition. Most likely, to put it succinctly and without any psychobabble, it beats the living crap out of a person. Such is the case with me, I'm afraid.

I've sensed that my heart has slowly numbed, not because I have wanted it to, but because it must so that I can function when those surprising and devastating times arise. It's a level of numbness that doesn't interfere with my ability to provide the necessary and needed care. Instead, it's a level of numbness that *allows* me to act with my heart and mind calmly and clearly when those things happen. It's a kind of buffer. It's a respite. It's a form of protection for me, who must go on despite the circumstances. And I genuinely believe it is from God and a gift.

God has given this gift to both our daughter and me, who has come in from out of state to be the daytime caregiver during this journey. But that's just one gift, one kind of gift. Last night, He gave another gift . . . a gift of unimaginable love. To set the stage for that one, let me set the table for it. Our marriage has been no different than anyone else's. It has not followed the path we thought it would when we were young and dumb, seeing the world through those rose-colored glasses. It's had its bumps, uglies, twists and turns, and everything else. It's sometimes been a challenging ride on this journey.   Last night, after cleaning up after a bed accident (after our daughter had gone to where she was staying), I went to say goodnight to my wife. Later on, I received a text from my daughter wanting to know if Mom was asleep yet after all the extra strain she had experienced from her accident. In response, I shared the following text with her (and some others) to offer an example of how sometimes God gifts us in special ways with perfect timing.

Not yet. I think she's just getting ready to. We just had a fantastic time together. Perhaps the best in all the 46 years we've been together. It was so beautiful. We laughed, we cried, and we prayed. And then the surprise of my life. She said, "I've always wondered what it would've been like if we had had a child together. I'll bet all the kids would've helped (we were a blended family).

Isn't that amazing? I shared with her that I've often thought the same thing, though it was never discussed. Talk about an extraordinary moment. It gave me chills, and the hair on my arms stood up. So beautiful. I think I saw the most incredible and beautiful smile I had ever seen from her that night.

At a time when I was beginning to feel that this old man's breaking heart was going to be in a terminal and unmendable condition, God gave me an incredible moment of mending, of healing, one that was a gift. And as I made that terrible and dreadful walk upstairs in the morning to see what I was going to find (a wife who had passed on or a wife who was breathing), there was just a bit of a lift to the feet as I did so . . . one that was courtesy of a healing moment from God last night. He is good.

Tiptoed in the Room

My son-in-law recently texted me a YouTube video of a song. He lives in California and knows all too well what transpires during a journey like the one we are traveling. He has experienced loss in his family. It was a lyrics video of a song written and sung by Chris Stapleton called "Joy of My Life." Perhaps before you read further, you would want to find it and play it while reading. It's worth your while. I've shared the lyrics below:

I tiptoed in the room
I know you got to have your rest
She says, "Come lay beside me"
"I been waitin' since you left"
She's sweet to me
Must be the luckiest man alive

TIPTOED IN THE ROOM

Did I tell you, baby
You are the joy of my life?
First time that I saw you, mmm
You took my breath away
I might not get to Heaven
But I walked with the angels that day
She takes me by the hand
I am the luckiest man alive
Did I tell you, baby
You are the joy of my life?
Some may have their riches
Some may have their worldly things
As long as I have you
I'll treasure each and every day
Just take me by the hand
I am the luckiest man alive
Did I tell you, baby
You are the joy of my life?
Did I tell you, baby
You are the joy of my life?

There's no more to say. What is here is sufficient. It speaks to the joy I feel after quietly entering the bedroom early each morning, uncertain about what I might find. Then, I can gaze upon the joy of my life lying on the bed and see that we will have the privilege of sharing another day.

Peace.

I Am NOT Going to Say Goodbye

Some weeks back, folks close to my inner circle knew that one of the things I was most deeply concerned about during this journey was the fact that I felt an inner uncertainty as to my wife's spiritual condition. I shared a bit of that earlier. I'll go into more detail here because of a remarkable outcome. She's always been a good person, a humble person, a simple person without wants, and a person who has neither lived in the past nor the future. She cares for others, most often putting their needs before hers. She is a gentle soul. To everyone's knowledge, she doesn't have an enemy in the world. In her formative years early in life, she was raised away from home in a Catholic school, and in later years, she attended an all-girls Catholic school. In her life, she's not been an active participant in church. So yes, as a committed Christian, I have prayed consistently (as well as inwardly bellyaching out of frustration) about the condition of her spiritual life as I perceived it. This has weighed particularly heavily on my heart for the past six weeks since we began this new chapter. My heart has ached about it, and there have been times when I wanted to yell out at God, "Come on, Man, let's get it done. Do something or teach me how to do something for this circumstance because she hasn't responded in ten years since I have been a committed Christ follower." I have been very fearful that she would die without knowing Jesus. And I know that would make saying goodbye so very painful when the time comes.

A good friend is one of the most discerning people I know. She also happens to be the wife of my pastor/friend/brother/mentor/and so on. Knowing of the situation and my concerns about Penny, she approached me a while back and shared something that turned out to be very special to me. Looking into my heart and soul through my eyes, she gently said, "Joe, it's easy and non-threatening. Ask her these two questions: *"You believe in Jesus, right?"* and *" You believe in what He did for the world and you, right?"* I stood there stunned at the ask's simplicity, the questions' calmness, and their non-threatening nature. So, later that evening, I shared them with my wife at a moment when I felt that the Lord had opened the door to her heart.

It's all on me. This one is. She responded to those questions immediately with a yes, a good solid yes—an "of course." Phew, I felt an immediate rush of relief. Later, it dawned on me that my concerns were more about me than of her. I had been too concerned that whatever I said to her or asked her had to be well thought-out and worded carefully, and the timing had to be just so. My mind was telling me, "It's *got to be just right.*" Right! I was more concerned about possible rejection or ridicule than her salvation. My fear of confrontation was in overdrive, as it has been throughout much of our marriage. The enormity of this mistake came to roost *after* I asked her those two questions. I remembered that in the past, I had "confronted" and then shared Jesus with two big, burly, macho, and very troubled and broken men who I knew, and I had done so without any fear or reservation. And they accepted and, in time, became very committed Christians. Why would I possibly fear a reaction from the woman I had been married to all these years? Duh—this was on me.

When she answered as she did, all anxiety left me. It went so fast I could almost feel the breeze it left as it flew from my heart. Since then, combined with a couple of major emotional meltdowns, I have noticed changes in my way of thinking about her and our relationship. One other thing stands out in those changes, and it's huge. My pastor/ friend/brother/mentor shared something very gently with me later when we discussed this.

> "Now you won't be saying goodbye. Now you'll be saying 'See you later.'"

He gently said, *"Now you won't be saying goodbye. Now you'll be saying 'See you later.'"* The thought of that makes me cry happy tears for a change, even in the face of the loss that is to come.

If God plans for her to leave this earth before I do, I can look at the situation through different eyes and with a contented heart. And I can do so not only because of what I have just shared but because I remember when I, too, answered those two questions (though they came in a different form) and accepted Jesus into my life, a life far from perfect. That may explain why one song speaks to me as it does. It means so very much to me. It's "Running Home" by Cochran & Co. and can be found on YouTube. I can't urge you enough to check it out.

It will be a joy to say, "I'll see you later," rather than just "Goodbye." God is good!

A Veritable Flood!

One definition of the word flood, according to Merriam-Webster's dictionary, is:

"an overwhelming quantity or volume."[6]

Well, that's certainly an accurate depiction of the word "flood" when it's used in the context of what happens when the dreaded "C" word becomes more than just a word but a harsh reality. Aside from the nastiness of the word in general, once it becomes a condition descriptor of a loved one, it's game over. It becomes sickeningly nasty, at the very least. It becomes much more authentic if that's possible. Once the word cancer is uttered by the doctor at the visit where uncertainty collides with reality, any doubt about how nasty the word is vanishes. The harshness of actual reality takes care of that.

That's when the elephant is in the room, clearly visible, fully felt, and experienced, and it becomes a fixture embedded in one's life from then on. As I have said since day one, it's best described that this elephant is not just technicolor but fluorescent. And IT WILL NOT GO AWAY! With its unwanted presence, the floods begin. The first flooding comes in the form of tears, tears of grief and loss, of shock and sorrow, of unbelief, and even of guilt. Then, the worst flooding begins. I experience random and spontaneous floods of emotions like never before. Some of mine have been so bad that I would willingly hop aboard Noah's ark to escape them.

Another flood that has come quickly and unexpectedly is the unwanted urgings of the demons holding space in my head and all the dark spaces they try to entice my mind to go to. They play dirty. They don't make nice at all. They're persistent. If you have any doubts, try spending five minutes of quiet time when you strive to avoid focusing on anything. It's challenging to do so. That's why I so easily fall into their traps. The demons know very well how to keep me stirred up. They are stirring the elephant into action. My mind doesn't rest. They see to that.

In some of the earlier chapters, I wrote about waves of emotions and feelings that flood my mind with a numbness that impacts my sense of well-being and robs me of peace and joy. Simply numbing me wrecks any sense of purpose and passion I have left. The numbing makes it difficult to function other than by instinct.

All of this said I have found some natural and positive floods. One is the veritable flood of people I have discovered who genuinely love me for who and what I am. No pretensions. Just me as I am. They've always been there, but it's different now that the elephant is in the room. They glow with the love they show through honest interest, compassion, empathy, prayers, kindness, and the shoulders and ears they offer. This isn't just any ordinary flood. This is a flood of whitecaps.

The last flood I'll share is the generosity of people, many of whom seem to have come out of the woodwork. I have had to be reminded to let people be generous toward me because *they don't have to help—they want to help.* They want to bring food, offer themselves up to do whatever needs to be done, or do amazing things anonymously. I have had to be reminded that these people are Jesus's feet and arms on earth. They *are* Jesus with skin on, and I must be humble, honest, and grateful. I mustn't say such things as "We got this" or "We're good" and the like. I must say such things as "Thank you from the bottom of our hearts" and a quiet "We so, so appreciate you and what you have done." The love, caring, and actions of compassionate others have come as a veritable flood.

And Just When I Thought . . .

This chapter might come across as disturbing to some. That would be normal (ugh, that word again!) because it shares some somewhat negative thoughts. And now, the "but" is the reality of this situation, albeit an unwanted and ugly truth. It's thoughts that are not often shared or spoken of. However, I would bet my bippy that it's held court in the minds of anyone experiencing, or who has experienced, the probable loss of a close loved one. I repeat, that would be normal.

I felt as if I had somewhat successfully (if there is such a thing) navigated the grieving process after first hearing the word "terminal" applied to Penny's condition. I experienced that process for what I thought was a long time . . . weeks and weeks. I couldn't think or talk about it without breaking down. And, of course, I couldn't get it out of my mind, so the grieving process that I was experiencing was not just constant, but to be truthful, it was horrible. I couldn't smile, I couldn't find joy, I couldn't feel happy about anything, and I couldn't find peace. Rugged is a good descriptor.

Then God orchestrated something I wrote about earlier . . . her acceptance and acknowledgment of Christ in her life and what it meant and stood for. At that point, I felt a welcomed relief from the harshness of the grieving process I was experiencing at the time. A significant burden had been lifted from my heart. I now knew we would ultimately be together after her passing and mine.

I started to smile at times. I could laugh occasionally. Sometimes, I could talk about the situation without becoming a blubbering mess. I wasn't a happy-go-lucky guy by a wide margin, but I *felt* a bit more like the old me. The weight of all that was happening didn't go away one iota. But it *seemed* that at least I was in a little bit of control of the mess that was me.

More importantly, I felt I could function somewhat despite the lingering numbness. I wasn't enjoying life by any stretch, but I was starting to find it more tolerable.

Then today arrived. When I thought I was a bit more like Joe again, I discovered interrupters to my well-being. I was having some rare, peaceful, quiet moments. They were quiet from outside distractions, but it was evident that my thoughts weren't silent at all. They were unpleasantly noisy as I discovered some things about me in this situation that I had been unaware of. I needed those few quiet moments to see them. The moments gave me time for introspection and the opportunity to see what was happening inside. It's stuff that I have kept tightly sequestered in the deeper recesses of my mind and my aching heart. I've been afraid to talk about them in any way other than a roundabout way. I think it was because I felt that they were scary thoughts.

At this moment, I see alone times, quiet times, non-focus times, and downtimes as culprits to my recently found sense of relief. Below the surface, like a pack of sharks on the prey, are those newly recognized thoughts and feelings: I am over-the-top frustrated, I have a strong sense of being mixed up, I am feeling lost and out of touch with reality, I have the desire to curl up and go away, and I am experiencing a sense of losing my mind. On top of this, I want to hide and isolate myself. That all tells me that I am on one enormous pity pot!

I think that much of the above stems from the fact that I am not giving grace to others as I should. For instance, some family members don't seem on board with what is happening. Maybe it's my failure to recognize that everyone grieves differently, not necessarily like I do. Or perhaps the absolute uncertainty of everything daily doesn't go away. Or maybe it's the giant elephant in the room—the one we all know is there but seem to avoid. At least so far. That elephant would be one word, "When?" Or put another way, "How long before the end?" Both are ugly questions we *WILL* have to face at some point, but when? Those questions' underlying subtlety and bluntness are perhaps the shadow in which those sharks swim below the surface.

So, when I thought things might improve, I realized they had changed. With that came a change in my grieving process. I'm sure there will be more.

Embrace the Suck

It was a different kind of evening. A friend came over to hold space with me. I'm pretty sure God planned it that way. He sent him over because He knew I needed to unravel a bit!

I was firmly entrenched in my newest pity pot, the one I just wrote about. I whined to him in my finest whiney voice, just how much this all sucks. At the center of it all was the "me" factor, as it usually is. I was on the throne of self-centered pity. I discovered this through some pointed comments on his part. I don't mind, and never have, being taken away from my comfort zone and tossed to the lions. But the basis for that has been that I needed to have some sense that there were four parts to the process: it should be somewhat temporary, it should usually be of my choosing, it would result in a predictable outcome, or it was something that I knew I could/would claim victory over. I was wound up when he just happened to drop by, and I shared the situation I had to deal with because Penny's health had evaporated any comfort zone I might have. It was completely different because none of the four criteria I imagined necessary for stepping out of my comfort zone were present. There is no new comfort zone to be found, and I emphasized in no uncertain terms how much it sucks.

My friend listened patiently. He smiled. And then, without the slightest hint of being snarky, he shared his thoughts about it in three short words. *"Embrace the suck!"* With that, I took the meaning to flip it off if I wanted or needed to. But I also had to recognize that this suck situation is not of my own doing. It won't go away; it will most likely escalate in nature, leaving me no choice but to embrace it if I want to remain sane, helpful, loving, kind, and useful.

We discussed things that I didn't want to discuss. But he knew that I needed to dump. I needed to be gently guided to those places so that I could see the wisdom of what he had shared with me—*embrace the suck*. I'm still processing that. I had previously shared my new dislike for the word normal, so he ended his offerings with a hearty laugh as he shared, *"I have to tell you that the 'n' word applies here."* I knew exactly what he meant!

There's some good news about that interaction. First, I didn't put my finest two-year-old imitation on and stamp my feet while saying, "But I don't want to embrace the suck," and I didn't hear (because I wouldn't have wanted to listen to it at that moment) "It will help you build character." My mom frequently said that to me as a kid (along with "This too shall pass"). I'm glad. Because had I heard it at that moment, I most likely would have said that I have enough character, thank you, and I don't need anymore, and this won't pass.

I'm glad we had that conversation. It's clear to me that there isn't any other option than to embrace the suck because none of this is in my control. It is all in God's hands. And it served to remind me once again that deep down, I do believe that He will never dish out too much suck.

> *What a stunning picture this gives us of God's amazing providence—His ability to look ahead, know exactly what is coming, and make provision for us before we even get there. He is not only a God who can help us handle our current issues and pressures but One who has already prepared comfort, help, and blessing for problems that aren't even on our horizon.*
>
> *~Nancy Leigh Demoss~*[7]

Anguish Is Real—Not Just a Word

I struggle with the thought of writing this. I don't know the tipping point that made me share it. The only thing I can think of is the obvious—writing equals catharsis for me, especially in these moments. Today, I experienced anguish like I never had before. Never. It was a pain in my heart, one I had never felt, and it wasn't physical pain. Even the word pain seems to pale in comparison to what I experienced. Anguish, as described by Merriam-Webster[8], is extreme pain, stress, and anxiety. That is anguish lite when compared to the anguish I felt today.

I cared for my wife this morning, attending to her many needs. The wounds on her butt needed cleaning and medication, which meant changing the adult diaper so that I could get to those areas. It also meant watching her wince in pain as she was rolled over onto her side so that it could be done. Then, she had to be gently prodded into doing her bed exercises, which any person in moderate distress could do easily. But not her. Not doing them could mean she could ultimately be vulnerable to other more dangerous issues. She needed to be coaxed into taking even a tiny amount of nourishment, which is hardly conducive to maintaining even a resemblance of everyday health. But that was all she could do. It was a pleasure to watch her reactions as I scratched the feet, which she said were itching, and then the legs; it was impossible to think that those same legs, now looking like sticks with skin on them, were the ones that carried a once vibrant, healthy woman. And, while every minute of all that I did was met with joy, comfort, and gratitude from her, every minute reminded me that our lives have been turned upside down and inside out, and neither of us will ever be the same again.

I saw and loved the joy and comfort that she felt from all that took place this morning, but that was all undermined by the fact that unless God delivers a miracle, even the condition she is in today will not remain the same. It will worsen with time. While doing my love work with her this morning, I felt the anguish welling inside me like a slow, ready-to-blow volcano. As it did, a verse came to mind, one my mom would share with me often when I was a kid.

> *"Don't let this throw you. You trust God, don't you? Trust me."*
> ~John 14:1 (MSG)

Yes, I know that. Yes, I believe that. But sometimes what I see and experience in the immediate time, such as this morning, makes that seem lame. Though it came to mind, the verse did nothing for me. As I felt the volcano readying itself to erupt, I had to go downstairs. The anguish today was horrible and very, very real. Why I couldn't share it with her, I don't know. Maybe it wasn't time yet. Perhaps it was that I didn't want to upset her. Maybe I was being selfish. Possibly, I couldn't do it out of fear that its uncontrollability would yield adverse effects that weren't appropriate at the time. Maybe I just wasn't ready. And most likely, I thought I had to protect her from it.

I thought about my aloneness as I experienced the anguish. Was there some macho within me that prevented me from reaching out to someone who would come and hold space with me as I wailed uncontrollably, someone who would have to listen to the noises that came out of me that not even I had heard before? Someone whose shirt front would be soaked with the gushes of tears that poured out from my soul. Someone who would be able to withstand the shaking and almost convulsive and uncontrollable retching of my body as I cried. Someone who could just "be," holding space silently with me as I released what needed to be released, what couldn't be held back.

I lay in bed in the fetal position, hugging my soaking wet pillow with all my strength, and the emotional storm slowly left, wound down and worn out, all on its own. I realized I needed every bit of those moments to be alone through them. I needed to be alone with every bit of the pain. And all the tears. It was all as spontaneous as it was real, and there would have been no time for anyone to get here to be here. As I think about it, had there been someone, perhaps the moment, as ugly and painful as it was, would have been ruined. It certainly would have been different.

In the aftermath, I felt spent. My head hurt as if it had been squeezed in a vise. My heart was heavy as if weighed down by diving weights. My chest hurt from the explosive crying and wailing. And yet, I found some calm. Anguish is real. It's not just a word.

Gonna Be Okay

All moments in time, not just some, are special, except for our brokenness; we tend not always to acknowledge that. I'm certainly that way. I tend to categorize moments in time and then fit those moments into little boxes—this one to the "ugh" box, this one to the "awesome" box, this one to the "special" box, and so on. But I've been getting it wrong. All moments are special. Each one is a gift from God. Each one is here for just that instant and will never be seen again like life itself.

Going out these days, except for buying groceries, has its limitations. Someone must be with Penny, or at least in the house 24/7. There's no such thing as hanging out with buddies or going for coffee with someone, even when my head screams that I need to take a break from it all. And sometimes phone calls and texting don't quite cut it. I've always been a people guy who needs that real live face time and connection in my life.

I had the delight, privilege, and honor of having a wonderful community time at home last evening. A small group of men from church came together to break bread, be together, spend some focused time with God, and enjoy each other's unique company. I knew most of the unpleasant and hard stories that each man carries. One of the things I wanted to do to make the evening special for each of us was through music, my go-to medium often, and some other meaningful things.

I played, and we sang "You're Gonna Be Okay" by Brian and Jen Johnson. It's a Christian song that can be found on YouTube. However, when it was played, it was done so with a twist. Earlier, I printed out the lyrics to the song in first person, and we sang it with gusto in first person. It put an entirely new spin on the song. We could "own" the song differently than usual by singing it in the first person because it was so personalized. I was singing about me. John was singing about himself, and so on. It was a powerful and special moment for each of us. I don't know about the others, but I do know about me—I was reminded of a perspective I needed then—that despite my current circumstances, I'm gonna be okay. God has this, and me. I'm gonna be okay.

I'll Say Yes, Lord

That's what I want to say. That's what I hope I will always say when I know that God has spoken to me about something. It's the best response, really the only one, to God when He nudges me or speaks into my heart. But I haven't always done that, and I probably won't at times down the road. That's because there are still too many times when I figure *I have it all under control, know the right way, or know what's best for me.* When any of those "I figures" pop up (and they do more than I would like), I find myself in one or more of several different frames of mind: I'm pissed at God, I'm wrestling with Him, I'm bargaining with Him, I'm doubting Him, I'm trying to direct Him (Ha—see how far that gets!), or I'm arguing with Him. Sometimes, I am amazed at how much chutzpah and energy it takes to go to those places, yet I keep returning to them.

I often turn to music to speak to me. I seem to be wired to be responsive to messages in music. One song came to mind as I was processing my thoughts while trying not to listen to some onerous voices in my head today. I needed to hear it, and I found myself repeating it. I recommend you look it up on YouTube and listen to it as you digest what I'm sharing. The lyrics are simple and repetitive, but they packed a wallop for me when I needed to hear them. They reminded me of the man I should be—one who says "yes" to God, and not the man I so often am—the doubting, angry, directing, bargaining, and argumentative one. I'm referring to the song "I'll Say Yes" by The Brooklyn Tabernacle Choir.[9]

If I choose to say "Yes, Lord," I will find that I will have more confidence walking this unwanted journey my wife and I are on. I will trust

God and His will more about this whole thing. And I will recognize more clearly that He isn't about to lay any more weight on me than He knows I can carry and handle. He will protect me from myself if I just let Him—by saying, "Yes, Lord," and submitting myself (my heart) fully to Him. In my mind, just a mere sixteen inches away from my heart, I know that I can trust Him and that He will protect me, but I often find myself failing to lock that knowledge to my heart. Perhaps that is the Evil One messing with me and my yielding to being messed with.

In my most focused thinking/feeling moments, I have hummed the above to myself as I mouth the words, "I'll say yes, Lord," I know the feeling it gives me in those moments. It's a closeness to Him that is almost surreal. Those moments are moments of calmness, peacefulness, and joy. They are moments unfettered by evil or unhealthy thoughts. They are moments free of actions that say I was thinking of anything but "I'll say yes, Lord."

Tomorrow may well be an emotionally tumultuous day for me. I won't know until it comes. What I know now is that if I focus on the "yes" word, weathering that storm will be much easier than some days I have had in the past two and a half months. All I need to do is remember that. So now I'll practice once again: "I'll say yes, Lord."

It's Just Tough

One of my favorite places to stand and gaze when shopping is at the grocery store's meat counter. I don't know why I'm fascinated, but I know that the meat counter is one of the places in the store where I always feel like I am looking at perfection. All the different cuts of meat look beautiful to me. Gazing at them, my eyes and stomach tell me that I can prepare a wonderfully delicious meal with any cut of meat.

However, the awful truth is that good packaging and nice-looking displays don't always mean good meals will be the result. Sometimes, the meat that I buy is tough. I have gotten hooked more than once when purchasing a beautiful-looking steak. I always envision a sensually sizzling, beautiful steak with grill marks and one that smells wonderful when on the grill. But sometimes, it is hard to cut and worse to chew when served. Sometimes, I think shoe leather would have been easier to eat! It isn't enjoyable. It's dashed hopes and expectations! And it's just tough, literally and figuratively.

Dealing with people can sometimes be like eating beautiful but inedible, tough steaks. What's even more challenging for me is forgiving them. Sometimes, I find myself more willing to eat that shoe leather I spoke of than forgiving those others. This is true regarding close family members. And, in our case, it was especially true when the big "when" elephant was in the room, even though we didn't wish to acknowledge it.

IT'S JUST TOUGH

We're all watching our loved one wither before our eyes. It's heartbreaking. It isn't something we wanted to see or experience. We neither asked for nor wanted it, and it certainly wasn't planned. It isn't uncomfortable. It is downright painful. What was once a vibrant and self-sufficient woman is now a weakened, shriveling woman who needs constant care. And, because cancer has the knack of sucking every bit of vitality out of its victims, we are all aware that what it once was will never be again. That is why every single moment while she has all her mental faculties is so important. Her mind and her heart haven't been affected so far. And yet, there are those family members who, because of either denial or hardened hearts, don't choose to spend as much time with her as they might while she still has "good" days. They are the ones losing out.

I get angry about their not wanting to engage more than they do. I find it hard to understand. I have trouble buying that "they have their own lives to live" excuse. I have trouble understanding, "Well, we had plans." In those moments, I had trouble accepting that every person grieves differently. I sometimes have a lot of trouble with the BS I hear. It's their mom for crying out loud. Where's the love? Where's the concern? Where in the hell are their hearts? And thus, I have a lot of trouble forgiving. I find myself reminding myself that Jesus gave the absolute best modeling of forgiveness ever when He had the snot beaten out of Him and was hung on the cross, and He cried out as written in Luke 23:34 "Father, forgive them; they don't know what they're doing." Why can't I do that?

Because it's tough to want to follow or see that model, it's tough knowing that eventually, when cancer wins, I will need to lean into that modeling even more than I can imagine, lest I turn into that unpalatable piece of shoe leather myself.

Yes, It Sometimes Feels Like My Freaking Head Is Exploding!

When I began journaling what I was experiencing in both my heart and mind at the beginning of this journey, I did so from one perspective: I felt strongly that if anyone were to benefit from what I was sharing, it would need to be as raw and real as it was when I experienced it. Cancer is not a nice, user-friendly disease. Not to the patient. Not to the caretakers. And certainly not to the family.

The title probably sounds like something coming from a whiney little bitch. And, yes, today, for the most part, I am that whiney little bitch. The fact is, I don't care what anyone thinks about it. I have tried to look at myself rationally today, but I've not seen much—very little. I've tried to embrace the suck, and today I am just beaten down enough not even to want to try. Today, I am really on a roll because I hate myself for the way I'm thinking and for what I'm feeling. They both go hand in hand. So, what are they?

I don't feel like loving some of those in the inner circle today . . . other than the one I'm trying to help the most, the one wasting away in front of me. I don't feel the strength nor the desire to extend any grace to the ones who are pissing me off so regularly. They seem dismissive, almost narcissistic, I believe, and they think they are always right. Just ask them. They are manipulative. And the "care" they show is just that—a show so that they don't look bad (so they think) in the eyes of others. They are the "we're all on the same page" people whose pages are from different books.

So today has been a day when my head feels like it is freaking exploding. For a good part of the day, my anxiety has been over the top high because I sense that it's time to ask some hard questions of the person at the center of all of this—the one who is lying in discomfort on the bed 95 percent of the time. Hard questions about where her head is about her situation—legitimate questions because I don't know exactly what she is thinking about now and in the future. She has spent her life keeping personal thoughts close to her chest. And now it's very frustrating. It's like trying to know what I don't know. Such things as knowing what to do, when to do it, and how to do it—as each relates explicitly to her desire to fight this or not, her willingness to try to maintain the status quo, or (God forbid) her desire to let go. Some visible evidence has led me to think that there's a bit of all three in her thinking, which has become confusing. Given her lack of direct expression, there has been a series of mixed signals, and the resultant confusion has manifested itself to the point where I feel that I need to know what I don't know.

Perhaps the others in the close circle think or feel the same way. Maybe they don't know what to do, how to ask, how to act, or even know what they don't know. All I know is that, as I said above, the same page thing isn't working well, and the result is turmoil and drama that isn't wanted, necessary, or needed. It is clear to me that I don't do well with either. Living with chaos and drama isn't something I'm good with at all. As you correctly assume from reading this, I don't handle it well. And again, it makes my head feel as if it's exploding.

Here's what's going on with all of that as I see it. I need to find some grace because we, not just I, have been pushed to a limit we never saw coming, the result of which are strong reactions, some not always the best. I sense that some of my close friends would say, "That's normal." Today I have forgotten all about embracing the suck. Instead, I have allowed the suck to own me. As I think about it, I've been ignoring the fact that Satan loves to pick on my weaknesses and blow them all out of proportion so that I can become the hot mess that I am right now. No wonder my head feels like it's exploding.

I don't like myself one iota when I am like this. I think God didn't make me like this, and it confounds me why I get this way. The more I think, the more I dislike myself, and the more that happens, the more my head feels like it's going "poof." I'm not used to this at all. I'm not sure I've been here before, at least to this degree. It scares me because I sense I'm losing it, and then I get off on that tangent. And then I drift to what I imagine God might be saying: "Hey dummy, where do you think I am in all of this?" The scary part is that there are moments when I am not quite sure where He is. And that starts another cycle. And the explosion continues.

I have said much about what I don't know in my rambling. What I do know, however, is that I am down to strictly basics for the moment. I know I can't stop putting one foot before the other. I must accept that I must forgive myself for thinking crazy because if I don't, I won't be able to forgive others for their crazy thinking. I know it won't last because nothing ever does except God's love (directly and through others). And I know this has not been the first time I have felt like my head is exploding, and I believe in history enough to think it won't be the last. I know that I must trust God on that one! Right now, that's not easy. Oops, careful there—I don't want to start yet another cycle.

One Last Dance

Ten days have passed since the last post, yet it seems like yesterday. A lot has been going on. All my focus has been on her, and all my time has been spent with her in the hospital. My bride's condition during that time has deteriorated. Physically, she is no longer anywhere near the woman she was. But her heart is the same, as is her mind. She's all out of "oomph" now. There's no gas left in the tank. It's a time we all knew would come, but we never wanted to see it.

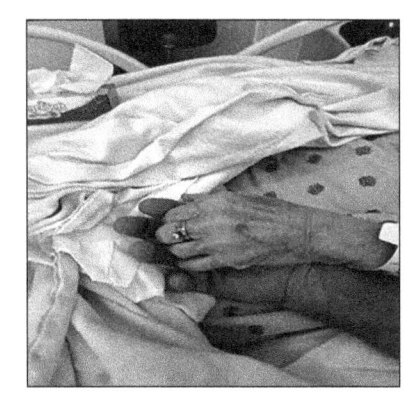

I sat next to her bed in the hospital the other night. I've often been sitting there by her side, usually holding hands. I can't sleep most nights, but sitting there holding a hand that wants to be held negates the longing to sleep. We both find extraordinary peace in it. It's special, even with the often-long periods when no words are spoken. Holding hands and the "being" feeling that comes with it is sufficient. And meaningful. And important. We are indeed one in those moments.

As we held hands the other night, I started to laugh because of a scene that passed through my mind. She was awake and aware then, asking me why I laughed. I told her, "Because I'm a silly old man," and we laughed. Then I explained why I had said that. I shared that the handholding reminded me of the many times we had danced. You see, I love to dance, and I've always known that I dance as well as I can weave oriental rugs—something I do not know about. With seven kids and multiple cousins over the years, the family has had many wedding receptions. I graced them with my finest non-Fred Astaire dance moves, a good portion of which were booze-assisted. I could make those legs fly in ways they were never meant to move. And poor Penny... though I couldn't always see her eyes rolling during those times, I know they did. She had real class. She never told me to please go sit down!

I told her how much fun those times were for me—being with her and dancing my butt off. Then I told her why I was laughing. I shared how much, at that moment, I would give to have one last dance with her. That's when she laughed! We talked about how I would have to pick her up off the bed and hold her close with her feet off the ground (because by that point, she could no longer stand up) and swirl around the hospital room to some imaginary jitterbug music. I could picture it—even knowing how impossible it would be because I couldn't even pick her up, let alone dance. The visuals we both saw were awesomely crazy and wonderful simultaneously.

One last dance.

> "Life isn't finding shelter in the storm. It's about learning to dance in the rain."
>
> Sherrilyn Kenyon[10]

The First Homecoming

Yesterday was homecoming day—the first of two. The preparations were all made, and the wait began for my beautiful bride to arrive home from the hospital for one last time. No one was more anxious to be home than she was. This is her place; since 1977, it's been her roots and rock. It's where she belongs.

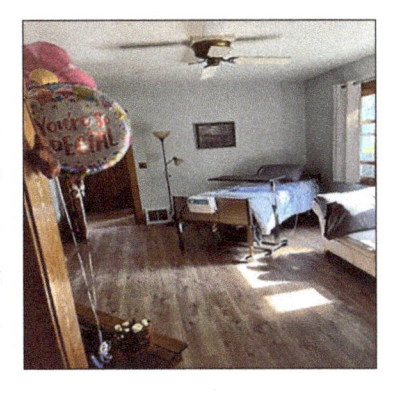

As an aside, it's the place I often wanted to escape from, to move from—or sometimes a case of "run away from"? My hope had always been to retire to a warmer place. Hers said this was the warmest place because that's where the family is. Her roots were stronger than mine, and here we are . . . right where we belong. This is what makes this homecoming so special. This is now a happy homecoming, despite the underlying grief of knowing that this homecoming is of shorter duration than we would like. Thus, it is a calming homecoming, a beautiful homecoming. It's exactly where we belong.

It's the first of two homecomings, and its goal is to ease her toward her second and final homecoming when she is released from our arms and goes to lay in the arms of Jesus.

What beautiful homecomings—this, the first one, and then the expected one.

THE HARDEST PART
IS WHEN FAMILY GATHERS TO SAY GOODBYE ONE LAST TIME

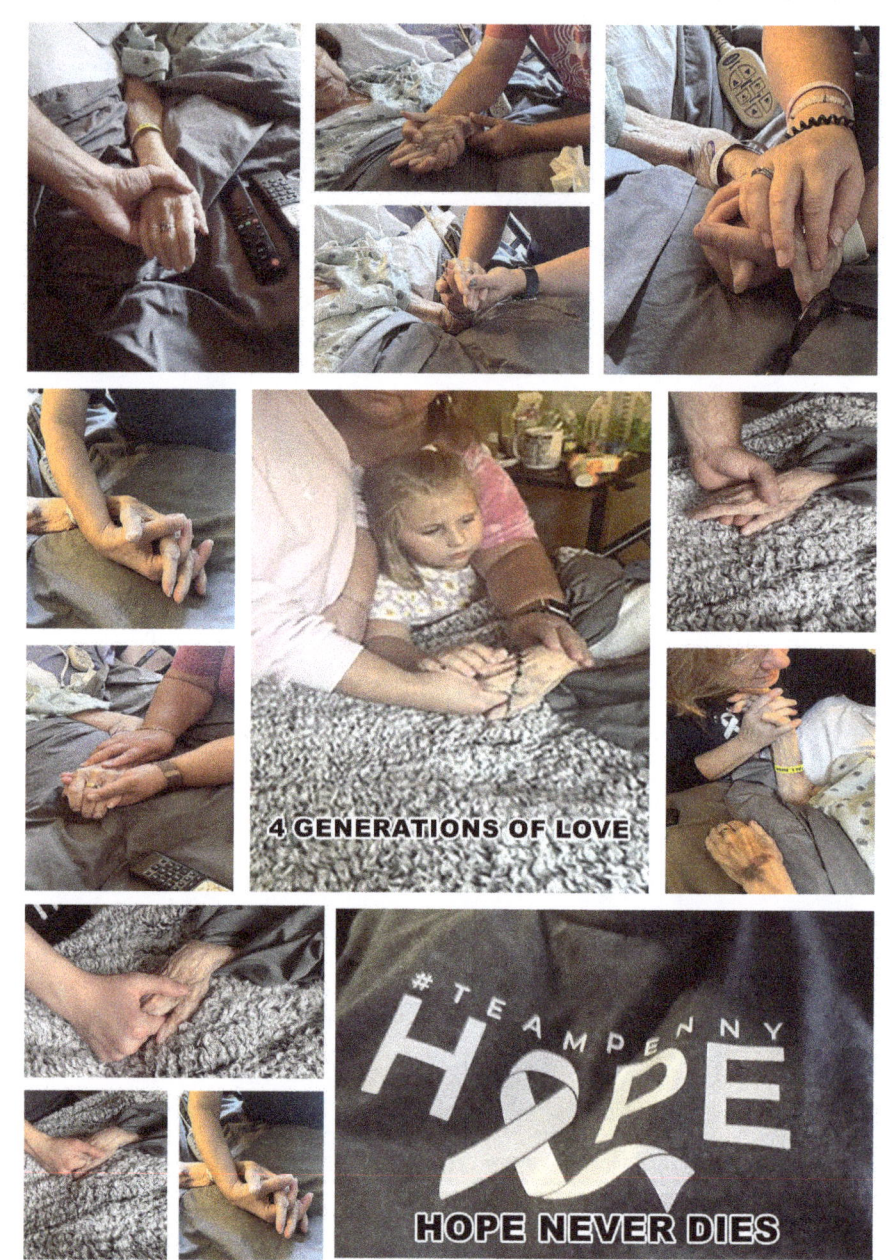

4 GENERATIONS OF LOVE

#TEAMPENNY
HOPE
HOPE NEVER DIES

THE HARDEST PART
IS WHEN FAMILY GATHERS TO SAY GOODBYE ONE LAST TIME

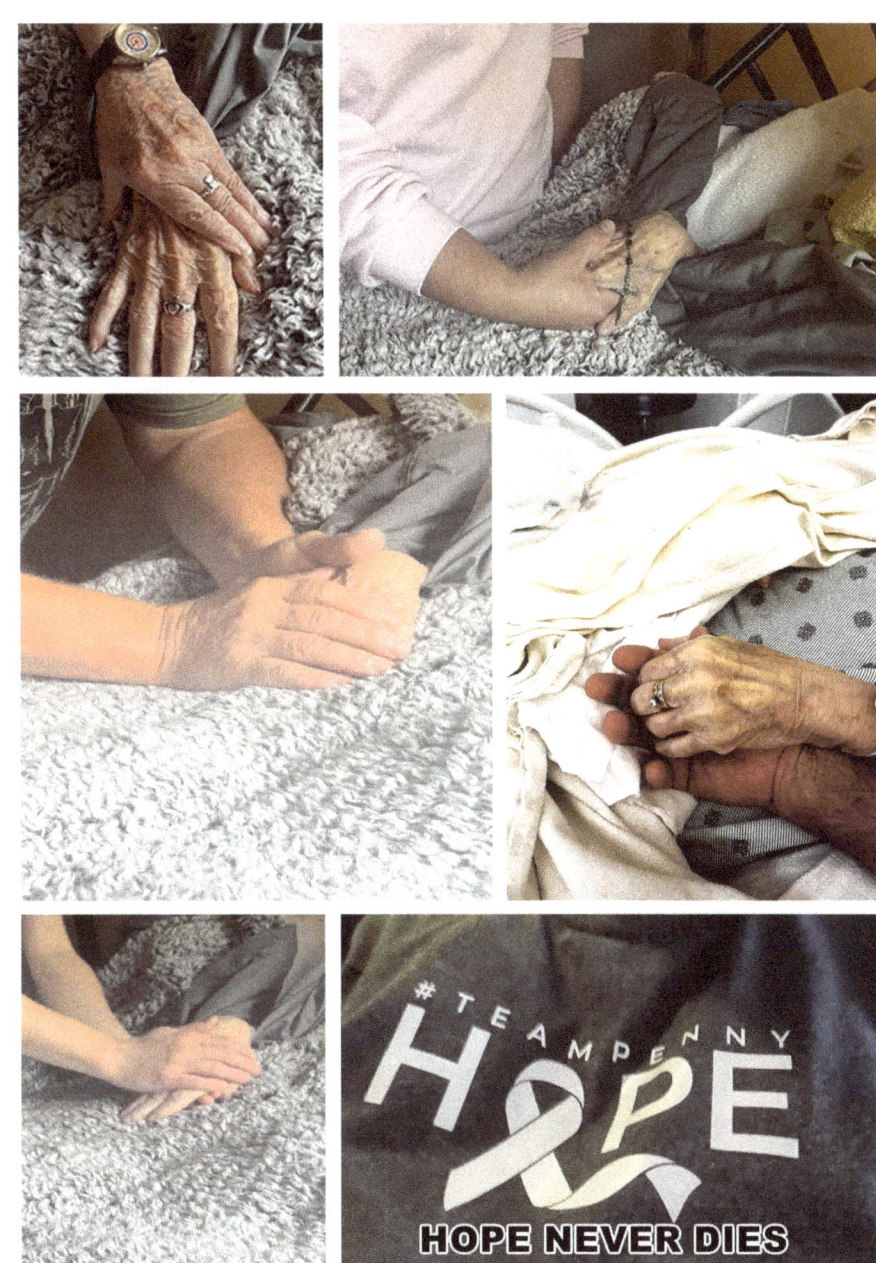

The Lowest Point

The family, the kids, their spouses, and their children had been summoned to the house late that night because the hospice caregiver was en route. She had been called per the grim protocol that hospice had shared with us. There were signs that the end was imminent. We called because there was little doubt that she was on the edge of passing according to all the visible indicators.

There is no way to adequately express the hopelessness each family member felt as they gathered in a mixture of hushed tones and eerie silence in the living room where her hospice bed was. The unspoken message carried by each face gathered there was universal. In our individual ways, we were painfully waiting. We were waiting for the thing we didn't want and would give anything if only we could reverse it—her last breath. Eventually, only each set of eyes spoke.

> We were waiting for the thing we didn't want and would give anything if only we could reverse it—her last breath. Eventually, only each set of eyes spoke.

During that time, the most horrible thing that could happen happened. Without going into detail other than to say I had experienced one a few years back, it was clear to me that I was having a mini-stroke. I remember the confusion I felt at that moment. I was experiencing not just a deep sense of loss in knowing that she would pass on at any moment but a repulsive shock over what was happening to me. This couldn't be—this was *not* the time for this—the family didn't need this with the load they were already bearing. And me—it elevated the sense of hopelessness I was already experiencing; I could bear no more.

THE LOWEST POINT

I tried to remain silent as I sat alongside the bed while holding her hand. I remember saying to myself, "I cannot possibly leave your side." I was also convinced that I *had* to be there for the kids in their time of despair. I *had* to be the strong one. It didn't work; the symptoms increased, and I knew my mind was working as poorly as my leg, arm, and face. I finally whispered to my daughter sitting next to me what was happening, and the rest was a blur. She's a nurse practitioner, and that side of her kicked in. Before I knew it, the paramedics were there, and I was in the back of the ambulance headed toward the emergency room, where I was admitted. I can find no words to describe the depth of the anguish I was experiencing knowing that I was not with Penny in her final moments. All I could think about was that this was the capstone of a forty-six-year run where I had all too often not been there for her. It mattered not that we had done our business during her final months and that all was forgiven.

I didn't know it, but my daughter had shared the current situation with the hospital personnel so that they could keep a close eye on me. I didn't realize at the time the depth of the abyss of despair I was in. At one point, my pastor, a very close friend, came to my bedside. I don't think there was any conversation, and I don't recall any. I know that I was in a very primal mode, curled up in a tight fetal position, completely covered in blankets as if I were in a cocoon. And I was rocking there in the safety of my space. I clutched his extended arm in a grip that must have conveyed the message, "You can't go," as I wailed uncontrollably for what seemed like forever. He silently held space for me as I had the lock grip on his arm in the worst ever moments of my life. I later recognized those moments of space he extended to me as the most profound expression of love a man can give to another.

I recall how exhausted and completely drained I was from such deep and uncontrollable emotions. There was nothing left for me. I slept deeply. That didn't last long because an endless line of doctors and technicians attended to me, ran tests, and checked me out. After I was released, I learned that everything regarding my care was "pushed." Being aware of the circumstances at home, they wanted to do everything as expeditiously as possible so that if what I had was minor enough, I could be safely released to be home with my bride and family.

Early in the morning, I was sleeping when the shuffling of feet awakened me, the privacy curtain being pulled back, and a voice that said, "Dad." Looking through the fog, I saw my three daughters accompanied by my pastor/friend. By the looks on the girl's faces and the presence of my pastor buddy, I instinctively knew what was to come. I was right. The girls stood there in obvious grief as my friend quietly and compassionately told me that Penny had died. I was devastated, but an odd thing happened. I found some strength in an unusual way. And I also felt a sense of peace even with the finality that came with the news. I found myself going back to a realization I had come to during the month ahead of her death. Because she knew Jesus, I wouldn't have to say goodbye. It was now "See you later," and I could envision a reunion down the road. I will be with her for eternity. Our time together here, though forty-six years in duration, was but a quick visit in the grand scheme of things.

This was all written retroactively. At the lowest point in my life, until this present time, I couldn't handle writing about this specific portion of my grief journey. Even now, as I finish editing it to share it, I am deeply emotional, reliving that time, which still brings anguish. But now I feel prepared to receive whatever amount of catharsis from writing it brings. I embrace it.

It's Not Goodbye

Today, I stand on the rock alone, looking toward heaven, as I muddle through the process of not saying goodbye but of saying, "See you later, baby girl." The rock is the foundation we built together, with plenty of mistakes, cracks, blemishes, nooks, and crannies. But it was our rock, and I believe it's the rock that God put in our paths so that we would find it together, join, and then live, love, and grow together. And that rock was strong despite the mistakes, cracks, blemishes, nooks, and crannies. It stood the test of time, forty-six years' worth. It took a beating. And yet it lasted. The rock is still here, though I am alone standing on it. It's a place that now belongs to me alone, and it will welcome me until it is my turn to go home to be with the one holding out her welcoming hand to me . . . my baby girl of forty-six years.

See you later, baby girl.

The Day That No One Wants

It's the day the grass isn't mowed, and the dandelions are left alone. It's the day the landscape is disturbed by a rectangular hole with a tent shading it, folding chairs carefully placed near it. It's the day no one wants.

It's a resting place—her earthly resting place. We must have her funeral, the one that no one wanted. That rectangular hole is hers. Her remains are there, but her heart is with us all as we each, in our way, try to find memories of happier times. Our only absolute comfort comes from the fact that she is resting in the arms of Jesus, whole once again.

It's the end of a forty-six-year physical relationship. Now, it becomes a mental relationship as I move on without her. It's the day that forces a new beginning for me, which I never wanted. It becomes different because it is different. I will become different. The kids will as well. It's not our choice.

It's the day that no one wants.

> "Have you ever lost someone you love and wanted one more conversation, one more chance to make up for the time when you thought they would be here forever? If so, then you know you can go your whole life collecting days, and none will outweigh the one you wish you had back."
>
> ~ Mitch Albom~[11]

We Rode the Horse Together

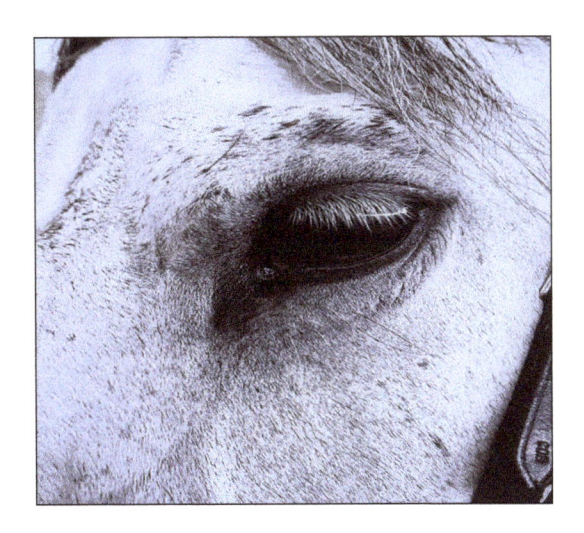

We rode the horse together, her and me,
To places far and wide,
For 46 years, we rode the horse,
Me and my beautiful bride.

It wasn't always pretty all the time we rode.
At times, the trail was rugged or steep,
And dirty and messy as well,
But it was our trail, our very own to keep.

That horse was our ride through the years we had,
It's the one we chose to ride.
And even with all its imperfections,
We gutted it through, me and my bride.

UNDONE

The horse became tired and worn and grey,
The same as us riding along,
It carried its load of two much in love,
Because me and my bride belonged.

We rode that horse together,
The two of us, her and me.
But now its load is lighter,
Because the only rider is me.

~Joe Miller~

What Now?

It's past us now—the day that nobody wanted. The tasks, mostly unpleasant but necessary, the calls that had to be made, and the arrangements that came were behind us. Everything, except some lingering questions, some important, some not so much.

The days are different now. The quiet of before seems even quieter. Things that once seemed urgent aren't all that urgent anymore. The stillness is stiller. The emptiness of the space around me seems even more hollow than before the day nobody wanted.

Gatherings are different. Each brings a different perspective to the present time because each was affected differently by that day. And those gatherings are now quieter, more subdued. Decisions that must be made are decisions that had no cause to be made before. Memories jump out of nowhere and at any time, and emotions are edgier.

So, what now? No one knows the answer because we are all facing a new normal. From now on, a different past, a changed past, will be built, and only time will tell what that will look like. Things will be considered differently because there will be one less person to throw their perspective into the mix.

Yep, a new normal is on the way.

PART 3
Moving On— Dance with the Limp

You will lose someone you can't live without, and your heart will be badly broken, and the bad news is that you never completely get over the loss of your beloved. But this is also the good news. They live forever in your broken heart that doesn't seal back up. And you come through. It's like having a broken leg that never heals perfectly—that still hurts when the weather gets cold, but you learn to dance with the limp.

~ANNE LAMOTT~[12]

As soon as the vault containing her casket was lowered into the ground, I knew. As hard as it was to accept, I knew that the word " different " took on a whole new meaning. When it popped into my mind as I watched the vault slowly lower, the word became almost an enemy. I wanted to run from it or, at best, push it away. I certainly didn't want to face it. I knew that it was reality and would become the norm (as if it wasn't already). And yet I mentally tried to find even the tiniest glimmer of hope that "different" wouldn't be all that bad. But everything within me was dark. There was no glimmer of hope. Reality was the only thing I could see, but it pierced me like a distorted dagger. I could not find that glimmer of hope I so desperately wanted.

I sat there, unable to stifle the questions that entered my mind. They were as numerous as the tears streaming down my face into my lap. How was I, a guy who always seemed to have an answer, a guy whose mom always called me "the happy little optimist," possibly going to navigate "different"? What would it be like? What would it look like? How would it happen? What would the results of this new way be? What would it do to me? Would I ever be able to adjust? If so, how? Or could I?

I knew nothing would ever be the same, which made it all so different. Yet, as out of place as they were, the questions ushered me into a whole new reality of life. It mattered not that it was unknown territory, but it was territory.

Then, a thought that was just as real soothed my broken heart. Though it was broken, nothing could ever take my memories of her from it. And I knew that no matter what, I would make it. I would go on. It would be different, but I would continue because she was still with me—just as she wanted it. Because of that, I had to move on—if only one step at a time.

What we once enjoyed and deeply loved we can never lose, For all that we love deeply becomes a part of us.

~Helen Keller~[13]

And Then What?

Caught with the hand in the cookie jar of life. It's an empty feeling. Utterly unable to decide in a clutch situation (name it)? It's an empty feeling. It's an empty feeling when you can't find the words to share with someone experiencing a painful time in their life. That empty feeling is one of numbness—of the mind and, in some cases, the heart and soul. It's a blank, a void, and an uneasy feeling. It's often a feeling we aren't used to because the situations that create it are random, few and far between. And it's something that we indeed don't "practice" for. We feel hollow, dry, empty, and uncomfortable in those moments.

The death of a loved one produces the same feelings, magnified by the knowledge that the situation is permanent. Death can't be undone. It can't be reversed. And the numbness is deep and profound within the soul. And I believe it is worse when one has witnessed and been a part of the process of the death of a loved one, the slow withering away of a once beautiful and vibrant person into a skeletal shell of what the person once was. It's horrible, close to being inhumane. The knowledge of the impending death does little to blunt the feeling of helplessness and hopelessness that takes place while watching it happen. And once the death occurs, the incredible sense of emptiness sets in.

The emptiness brings with it an equally strong feeling of loneliness. While quiet times were once a friend, an opportunity to be alone away from the noise of life, now they become the enemy. Those times bring with them memories, some of which are special, so one could massage the mind with their pleasantness. But sometimes, the memories spark moments of regret and shame from the awareness that there were blown opportunities to be more loving and kinder along the way. There were situations and words that one would give anything to change or take back. Then, those remembered past actions bring an almost unbearable feeling of guilt.

I find myself saying, "Now what?" or "What's next?" I keep seeing the light, but I still feel empty and hollow. I smile because I know how to, not because I want to or must. I smile, desperately trying not to cry. I go vertical to the God I believe in and try to trust that He's in control and that He will protect me and provide for my needs. I know I can lean into Him and should do so, but it is hard because I feel drained, empty, and hollow, and at times, I just don't want to.

Over the past years, I've often shared the words "be strong" with others who have faced difficulties. Now I know, as I wonder what's next, that I, too, must be strong, particularly when I don't want to or feel that I can't. I'm glad I lean into music as much as I do because I often find a sense of calm. There's a song that has been a go-to of mine a lot recently. It's "You're Gonna Be Okay" by Brian and Jenn Johnson. It's a Christian song you can find a lyrics version to it (recommended) on YouTube.

And then what? I'm simply praying that I'm gonna be okay.

Empty Space, Time, and Heart

I can't imagine hanging empty picture frames on my walls. How would it look? How would it feel? Would it make any sense? What would it mean? What could be done to make it right? Would whatever that is change anything?

It's been two weeks since she died. She, my bride of forty-six years. That's a lot of years. Some of those times were good, some were not so good, some were great, and some were just downright awful. We stuck it through just as we should have. The picture frames of who we were as a couple were full. There was something to see by anyone who cared to look.

Now, the picture frames of our life together are empty. Oh, I have the memories they made. But while memories are warm and wonderful, they lack the passion of their sources. Now, there's empty space, empty time, and an empty heart.

Each will have to be filled over time. They can't remain empty. It took a lot to fill them over the forty-six years we had, and I know that time, effort, and faith will help me to try to fill those frames again. But I also know that while the frames will look the same, the pictures within them will not. Each will be different.

> "We carry around in our heads these pictures of what our lives are supposed to look like, painted by the brush of our intentions. It's the great, deep secret of humanity that in the end none of our lives look the way we thought they would. As much as we wish to believe otherwise, most of life is a reaction to circumstances."
>
> ~ Richard Paul Evans~[14]

Memory Lane

Going down memory lane can be a delightful, fun time. Many of us, if not all, enjoy looking back at our good memories. Those are the places that bring chuckles and laughter and smiles as we embrace the happiest times in our lives. Warm fuzzies are how we should feel as we return to those places. We embrace that trip, and purposely going there is common. It's a place we know and like. It's like looking in the rear-view mirror of our lives to relive some of our past's beauty and good times.

The grief process also includes a trip down memory lane. We relive those special times, places, and things we experienced with the loved one we have lost to death. Though the smiles are coated with a sadness only imagined by those who haven't tasted it yet, they are still smiles. They are welcome smiles because they help to blunt the pain left by the loss.

But there is another aspect of those trips down memory lane that is far from pleasant. It brings with it some unwanted negative feelings, such as guilt, shame, regret, and the self-directed anger that arises out of those feelings. There is no happiness or joy in that trip. It's like looking in your rear-view mirror and seeing nothing but darkness.

The uninvited inter-relational thoughts that come to mind in that trip include plentiful "if-only" and a bunch of "should haves," "would haves," and "could haves." Each of those brings a special type of self-denigration that weighs heavily on the heart. They draw one's focus to those unpleasant (and hurtful) things about oneself that we would rather not revisit. They upset our belief (good or bad) that the past is the past.

I doubt that either of those glances into the rear-view mirror can ever be avoided. After all, as humans, we seem wired to take those two distinct journeys down memory lane throughout our lives, whether we wish to or not. But when they both co-join during the grieving process, I think it's different. With death comes the finality that no apologies can be made for those things that haunt one. One can only go to God for forgiveness and the strength to forgive oneself. When you get a moment, check out a YouTube lyrics video called "Rain in the Rearview" by Anne Wilson. It spoke to me.

> **With death comes the finality that no apologies can be made for those things that haunt one.**

The Faucets That Are My Eyes

It's crazy, just crazy. Sometimes, there's a day when I am fully present in the moment, and something will pop up right out of the blue. And then everything changes almost immediately. That happened today. It was unexpected, powerful, vivid, and real. It caused the faucets that show up in my eyes in moments like this to pour as if turned on full blast. It didn't matter that others were around. Reservedness or stoicism went by the wayside as if they had a will of their own–eager to escape, leaving me nakedly vulnerable. There was no control over them as they left me. It was one of those spontaneous, unplanned trips down memory lane. It was a result of outside stimulation. It was confusing because it produced joy and pain simultaneously, not separately, each vying for attention. It was like crying out of happiness from fixing a relationship and a conflict, crying out of anger for breaking it in the first place. (This is too good to pass up for a lyrics writer—" vying to cry," perhaps?)

I had been driving and listening to the radio when Clapton's "Wonderful Tonight" came on. It's an icon of the music world and perhaps holds the record for most used as part of wedding receptions. Instead of changing stations, I opted to hear it out. I cranked the volume up. Immediately, the song brought back some tremendous memories of times when Penny and I would dance to it at the receptions where it was played. It seldom wasn't played at one.

I relived the moments we had holding each other tightly as we effortlessly glided on air to the beauty of the song, entirely oblivious to those around us. It seemed as if we were as one in those special moments, joined in body, heart, and soul. In those few moments, we experienced a true revival of our love for each other and forgot everything else. As I listened to it, I felt as if, once again, I was holding her tightly and the world was ours. I could feel the movements and her body pressed into mine. I experienced joy as those memories filtered in.

But a cacophony of head noise injected itself into the moment as I started to feel tremendous sadness that this was a vivid dream or memory from a shattered mind. Those moments could never happen again. This sadness led to anger at the overriding thought that somehow, I had been robbed of something good, wholesome, and wonderful. The apparent fact that it wouldn't, or couldn't, ever happen again added to the sense of anger and sadness, and the faucets that are my eyes these days gushed without restraint.

Amidst the noise and the clutter of voices in my head, I concluded that conflicting emotions don't play well together and that, as a result, each clamor for the most attention in the mind of the one experiencing those emotions. And I found that it's not terminal, nor is it permanent. But it is real—very, very real when vivid fantasy collides with reality.

Just as She Would Have It

F amily is a gathering of hearts of all sizes and ages that span four-fifths of a century. One is on the cusp of leaving the womb up to the eighty-year-old kid. The hearts and the bodies surrounding them are all uniquely different yet somehow uniquely similar. Each one lost something special to them personally just three short weeks ago. Some lost their mother-in-law. One lost a great-grandma. Some lost a grandma. Some lost a mom. And one lost a wife. Each one lost a special woman who loved them deeply.

This gathering was joyful and happy. For a day, tears were replaced by smiles and laughter. Sad memories were set aside by fond memories from plenty of "remember whens." There were no agendas, dramas, or any underlying tension carried by differences. Any grief was set aside for an evening both wanted and needed. It was a time of unfettered unity and family love that filled that space. Conversations were open and free, without anything hindering a healthy family relationship.

So, there we were, many different people gathered into one space with one purpose—to have the kind of gathering so reminiscent of those many times when she was present with us. It was just as she would have it.

A Different Kind of Visit

Quiet. Serene. Beautiful in its way. It's not a place I would typically go to. Until now. It's a little longer than three weeks ago when I last spoke to my wife or heard her talk to me. The last words I heard from her lips were, "I love you too." Then, those lips were silenced a bit later as she passed from this life to move to her heavenly home.

I'll see her again one day when God sees fit to take me from my earthly home when He deems my work done. In the meantime, I am relegated to seeing and hearing her only through memories. Now, the only option is one that I've never had before. I must make a different kind of visit, a visit to that place where her earthly body rests, now at peace.

I did just that yesterday. It was my first visit. I thought it would be strange. It wasn't. I thought that I wouldn't be able to handle it. I did. It was a visit different from any visit I have ever made anywhere. I visited her final resting spot in the respectful quiet that perhaps only a cemetery can create. It was a different kind of visit.

I shared from my heart some things she wouldn't hear. But she heard. I felt welcomed and wanted in that space. I felt I belonged. Strangely, I thought we were still as one as I shared my love for her over a plot of ground. And we are still as one because death can't steal one's heart. I wish she could have seen my smile as I processed that thought. Perhaps she did because it was, after all, a different kind of visit.

Life Goes On

Life, like time, doesn't stop with the passing of a loved one. There are certainly times when, deep in my heart, I wish it would or could. But those are fleeting moments arising from the grieving process as I experience it in my unique way. Part of that process is learning to accept that the new reality, an emerging new normal, differs from what I knew. While on the grief journey during the caretaking process, the word "normal" took on a whole new meaning. What was normal *for* the process was not what I felt was normal for me because it was all new to me. It took a while to "get it"—that the grief process is, in fact, a good thing, a necessary thing, and a thing that ultimately needs to be embraced.

Now, in the life-goes-on process, a new normal becomes necessary because everything about life has changed as I experienced it my whole life. The differences run the gamut from simple change to change that often seems overwhelming. The circumstantially created need to create a new normal is not enjoyable. It's a change that is not wanted. It's change that comes with no choice but to make it. And it's change that is still wrapped with all the emotions that are a part of the whole loss of a loved one process. In short, I wouldn't say I like it, but I must embrace it because life goes on.

> **The circumstantially created need to create a new normal is not enjoyable.**

Creating that new normal looks intimidating because it means crawling out of the routine that was life as I knew it and building a new routine. It comes with a whole new array of questions, thoughts, and guesses about what lies ahead because the old routines have been disrupted or must be discarded. At times, it looks scary. At times, it looks impossible. At times, it just looks hard. But it always looks necessary because, after all, life goes on.

> *"And life goes on, which seems kind of strange and cruel when you're watching someone die."*
>
> ~ Melina Marchetta~[15]

I Wish, I Want

Right on the heels of writing about how life goes on and that the development of a new normal is necessary, today sucked in so many ways. Today, it was difficult even to attempt to embrace the suck. Today, I didn't try to embrace it. My heart couldn't. It was used up. Something cruel to my heart was holding space there. It was an awful case of "I wish, I want."

Here's what that looked like. We're in the fall now, and I've been enjoying the brilliant colors of the foliage this past week. Today was no different. The fall colors were brilliantly brilliant in the morning sun and the clear skies that came with it. I was all gaga as I saw the reds, yellows, oranges, and in-between tones of the foliage. Until. Until that is, I stopped to take a picture of a couple of oaks waving their unseen fingers at me and enticing me to capture their specialness. That's when the "I wish, I want" began. And they remained for most of the day. They functioned like an earworm does. For those who don't know what that is, it's the term that applies when you get a song in your head, and it stays there. You find yourself whistling it, humming it, and even singing it for hours, *and you can't seem to shake it.*

But today's earworm wasn't a song. Songs are usually happy earworms. Today's earworm wasn't happy. It was nasty. I found myself experiencing profound sadness because "today was a bitch." You see, I cracked when I snapped the above picture of the two golden oaks after seeing so much beauty before then. I wished my deceased wife could see them because she marveled and got such great joy from the fall colors. Her reactions were always as if she saw them for the first time. That was just like her. She consistently got so much joy out of so many of life's simple little things. It never took much to keep her joy button tickled!

My wish that she could see what I saw led to a bad case of the "I wants." The loud voice from the I Want choir screamed the impossible at me. "I want her back." I didn't want memories of those moments. They weren't good enough. I wanted her; my heart wanted her, but my mind kept reminding me how impossible that was. That didn't stop the earworm, resulting in a lot of crying, anger, and frustration.

The beauty of the foliage taught me a lesson today. The "I wish, I want" will happen, and I better not try to ignore them or pretend they aren't there. That earworm is alive and well and will probably have a long life. Just like the suck, so perhaps I need to learn to embrace the earworm as well. I think that so long as I have a memory, it will be hanging around. I sense it's just part of the new normal that I'm not very fond of. I wish, I want.

Teamwork

A month has passed since my bride left to go home to be with Jesus. It's a month that's flown by except for the first week. That's a week that stood still. It was a week when emotions were at their highest. And their rawest. The week had to stand still so that I could process the shock and enormous sense of loss I was experiencing. After a month, I'm beginning to ever so slightly see through the fog of despair that has surrounded me like a cloak. I'm seeing some things a bit more clearly about the process of losing a loved one. One of my observations is about those who didn't die, the family unit.

"There is no I in teamwork." Does that sound familiar? I used it often during my years as a business owner to encourage the employees at every level to work as a team to achieve success on a project. Egos and agendas were left at the door. Compromises were welcomed. They were all rewarded upon achieving success because each had played a part in the success. It was a team effort. When it works, it's a profound thing to witness.

Unfortunately, it doesn't always work that way. I was saddened to see that happen in a deeply personal way when we were experiencing the pending death of our loved one. It was a hard pill to swallow, and frankly, it still pierces my heart. There were times when raw emotions, hidden agendas, opposing observations, and, yes, egos tended to bulldoze any semblance of team unity/team action. I learned that end-of-life situations can exacerbate even minor differences of opinion or thoughts about any situation, even simple matters, into rifts that can cause relational damage of the most hurtful kind.

I saw how hard it can be to set aside one's need to be right in every circumstance. It's hard to see another's perspective when one is so deeply pain-wracked over the death of a wife or a parent, even if that perspective might be a better, more appropriate perspective. It's particularly hard to set aside past wounds with another family member, wounds that often run deep, having never been previously resolved. It's hard to forgive some of those wounds. And it's difficult not to let present circumstances, with all its high-intensity feelings and raw emotions, govern reactions and behaviors.

The late-term dying process appropriately calls for unity. It's one time when family unity is absolutely needed. But I found that it may not happen. Emotions are at their rawest. Tempers are at their shortest. Pain is at its fullest. Inside, each care team member is experiencing the journey differently, living it differently, and hating it just as much as the others. It's a time when keeping the "I" out of teamwork is most difficult.

Hopefully, in our situation, the sometimes lack of teamwork wasn't apparent to my wife. I think that each of us was sensitive to the fact that even as sick as she was, she could pick up on any disharmony, no matter how well-veiled it might be. In that regard, there was an understanding among us all. Her burden was her illness. She didn't need any burden on top of that one. In all instances, it had to be a family-first mentality, not one "I" driven. As the dad, even though it was a blended family, I had to be the alpha dog. That wasn't always easy because I knew how easy it could be to get one's feelings hurt due to the high emotions. Sometimes, it felt like a juggling act with raw eggs.

Teamwork. There's no "I" in it.

Words Don't Sleep

Words, spoken or unspoken, don't sleep. They might be words shared or not shared out of love. Or they can be the less-than-kind words that one wishes could be taken back. Either way, I'm convinced they don't sleep, particularly in my case, when they were words that could have impacted our relationship. I'm finding that those words are louder now than when they were either said or not said.

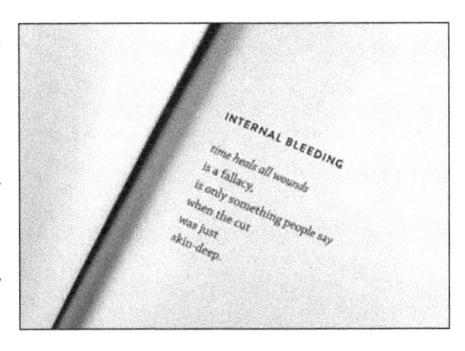

It's been over a month since she died. And as usual, unsettling surprises keep coming along. I know it's part of the grief process, but that doesn't change things. While some of the surprises are welcomed, others are not. All of them are a reminder to me that the grief process must run its course and that I have no control over that. It's the nature of the beast.

Though typically a heavy sleeper, I periodically wake up at night, rehashing some moment in time in our relationship. Maybe this is the nocturnal version of a memory, I don't know. During those twilight moments between deep sleep and awake, I find myself rehashing something I should have said to her or something I shouldn't have said. It might be a rehash of a recent or past conversation. There seems to be no pattern. Either way, it's an unsettling way to wake up.

Occasionally, that twilight time will be pleasant as I relive a conversation, or part of one, that brought us each some joy. Depending on the hazy memory arising in my subconscious at the time, I will lay there smiling at the memory or grieving more deeply. It can be a pleasant wake-up, or it can be a sad moment.

I thought about this and felt I needed to embrace a couple of truths I'm seeing. One is that words don't sleep. The other fact came from the mouth of Yogi Berra: "It ain't over until it's over." The words that don't sleep are more than just a paper cut, good or bad.

A Penny for Your Thoughts

I've been a regular customer of our local Starbucks for years. Years ago, I'd sit there for hours crafting and writing lyrics for songs I believed would someday become hits. If I tried to write lyrics elsewhere, my mind wouldn't share its creative side with pen and paper. My home desk was an absolute dry gulch for writing back then.

During Penny's last three months, I would stop at the drive-thru window of that Starbucks to grab a cup on the way to or from the hospital. Maybe I was more aware of it because of being tossed into the role of caretaker, but I was thoroughly struck by the cheerfulness of the gals manning the drive-thru. And especially one. She's on the north side of middle age and a vibrant woman. One day, I mentioned to her how thankful I was that I would come there and consistently leave feeling a bit "up" from being there. I wanted to tell her why, but I started getting very choked up and said that one day, I would share why I had said that. At that moment, I couldn't share that I was spending my days watching my wife wither away and that the brief oasis of calm when I came for coffee was so needed and valued.

Fast-forward to a couple of weeks after we buried Penny. I had to step out of my grief to take care of some business I had been neglecting. On the way, I stopped at Starbucks, and the drive-thru line was horrendous, so I parked and went inside. There at the end cap was the gal I had shared with earlier. I felt okay and emotionally secure at that instant, so I decided to share my earlier unspoken "why" with her.

But I wasn't as emotionally secure as I thought. When I began to tell her how grateful I was for the demeanor of all who had passed me coffee through the drive-thru, I started losing it. I tearfully shared how those brief moments had been like an oasis to me because of the heartbreak I was feeling from watching Penny deteriorate. Then I shared with her that Penny had finally succumbed to it, and I entirely lost it, as did the lady. So, we stood at the end cap, hugging each other as we bawled.

Now, fast forward to about six weeks from that tearful moment. One morning, I went through the drive-thru, and the same gal was manning the station. She was excited when she saw me and shared that just the day before, she had been talking with a customer in the same spot by the end cap where we had had our emotional time just a few weeks earlier. She went on to say she happened to look down at the floor, and a penny was lying there. She told me how she picked the penny up off the floor, and as she did so, she distinctly heard the words, "Tell him I'm alright." She got goosebumps relating the story to me, and I got them from hearing it. I still get them when I think of this story—and I cry.

A Bright Sunny Day, But . . .

It was a beautiful early fall day today. Crisp but not cold—fine enough for a sweater. Some of the trees are still giving the gift of fabulous fall colors. Those not bearing them have dropped theirs to the ground, where the familiar crunch of fallen leaves rewards those walking on them. The sun was out in full splendor, and there were some puffy clouds in the sky—the kind that reminded me of cotton candy or marshmallows. Yes, it was a bright sunny day, but . . .

It's been just a couple of days short of six weeks since she went to her final earthly resting place. It's park-like there. There are no stones or monuments, just plaques in their obsequious order placed on the ground. The wide open, well-trimmed grass areas dotted with mature trees strategically placed make it look more like a park than a cemetery. And the lack of noise makes it seem very serene and almost sacred in most areas—except for one spot—hers. That *is* a sacred space to me.

I went to that sacred space today, as I do regularly these days. It was emotional, as it always is. I go because I want to talk, and I need to talk. It always seems that there is so much that I need to share. And to hear. But I'll never be able to hear. So, I ramble on uninterrupted. It's catharsis for me. I can't leave those things I want to say unspoken. I must share, and it always brings me to tears and sobbing. Sometimes, I try to convince myself that I'll maintain my composure as if I must be the strong one, the rock. It never works, and I'm okay it doesn't . . . but I still foolishly try. She'd be okay with my emotions.

Those visits will never replace face-to-face conversations. It can't happen. But in my heart, I know the words spoken are heard. I don't know how, but they are. And I believe those visits to my sacred space are God's way of placing some healing balm on my wounded, broken heart. Yes, it was a bright sunny day, but . . .

Change

People react differently to change. I've always been a "go with the flow" kind of guy, so I've always taken change in stride until this grief journey thing. It upended most of what I had experienced in life as normal. Her diagnosis brought with it change. As did her death. New changes still occur, and new ones will emerge. Now, I'm bothered by the changes and the prospects of continuing changes that I suspect will come down the pike.

Some of the most prominent and glaring changes are 1) it's no longer us, but I; 2) it's no longer ours, but mine; and 3) it's no longer we, but me. Meals at a restaurant aren't the same because it's no longer us, just me. There are no more wonderful personal bonding moments over a meal that sits and gets cold because what is being shared is more important than interrupting it with a fork of food. It's no longer us as a couple who look forward to going to a party or a meal with another couple. The house we called home for so long is no longer ours, but rather mine—and I now wonder if it's a home anymore but rather just a house. An indefinable warmth once always present there is missing. These changes, which are real and unavoidable, bring a mixed bag of emotions with them. Loneliness is the one I find myself feeling most frequently.

Those three changes lend themselves to other changes I catch myself thinking about. They are generally future-orientated. Some examples are who will care for me if I get sick, certainly something not far from the realm of possibility at my age. Then there's another—what do I do when I'm here alone at night, and a medical crisis occurs in the middle of the night, and the house is empty except for myself? How do I manage that, particularly if I am incapacitated in some way? What if it's so bad that I can't call 911?

After years of having a trusty co-pilot in life's journey, learning to ask for help and lean on others when needed is a new change on the horizon. It's like swapping the reins from a one-horse ride to a wagon team—I will have to get used to calling out when the trail gets rough." Things like getting a ride to an outpatient procedure where I must have someone drive me?

Then there's the issue of managing the house and everything involved, including finances. I've always done some of it, and her other things–particularly finances–like paying bills. I've always hated paperwork and anything that smells like it, but now I must keep track of those things to avoid unwanted issues.

Those are all ordinary and mundane changes (though they are big for me). How about a change like who will protect me from myself? I've been known to make bonehead decisions or think stupidly about some things, but she was always my anchor. She always seemed to have the knack to do the next right thing when I didn't; while I didn't always like it, her judgment was always spot-on.

Thanks to some friends, I am taking a crash course in managing change–specifically, too much change, too soon. I've learned that a major change, such as the death of a spouse, creates a lot of underlying stress that I may not even be aware of or that I could deny is there or ignore. And I've been advised that it is *very* unwise to pile any self-made major changes on too soon because it has the propensity to mess with the head—things like selling the house and moving (especially if it's not a financial necessity). I've already entertained doing just that. But there are certain negative things that I neglected to see or didn't want to see. Fortunately, they were pointed out to me by some who care and speak the truth. It would have been a personal disaster had I acted on those thoughts without sharing them and then receiving sound advice, even if I didn't want to hear it.

CHANGE

A big change has been adjusting to a new and different daily routine. Now, everything is on me: shopping, when to do laundry, when to eat and what to fix, and how to adapt (if possible) to going out and eating alone when I feel the need for a change in routine. I'm not particularly eager to eat alone except when I eat lunch at work.

Speaking of work, when do I stop going to work? Yes, at eighty, I'm still working. It's all I've ever known; I'm scared of not working. If I do, what will take its place, and how will I adjust? Will I like the change or not? If I don't, how nasty will that sting? Will there be regrets?

Oh, there's more to be sure—lots of questions about change, what ifs, when, and how. Questions about my reactions to those yet-known changes will surely present themselves. How will I manage them and myself? That's a lot of stuff I don't know. What I DO know, however, is that I am not alone. I have an army of friends and a ton of support, and I better keep leaning into them, especially during this time of personal weakness. And I must keep my biggest supporter and cheerleader close by–God. He's got to remain my go-to consistently, especially during this time when I can be my own worst enemy. Keep my faith strong and let God worry about the change.

The Visit

Unlike most visits, this one is different. There isn't an invite to visit or a phone call to discuss the details, and there never will be. There's no concern about who else might be there when I arrive; my arrival time is a non-sequitur. They don't care when you arrive.

I visit my bride's grave site regularly. When I arrive, I'm looking for the landmark I've adopted to help me know where to park. I'd be in a real pickle if someone moved the lovely white wrought iron bench from under a tree near her plot. I know that if I park so I can look left to see the bench, it will be just a short walk to visit her earthly resting place. Everything seems so similar when walking through a cemetery, particularly with grave markers instead of headstones, regardless of my location. Yes, landmarks are needed.

The first few times I made that visit, it felt strange. Some fleeting thoughts were, "It's all wrong that I'm here—it shouldn't have to be this way," and "I've never wanted to be at a place so badly, but I dread what happens to me when I do go." I thought it might change, but it hasn't. I wonder if the grass seed planted on the bare soil of the stark rectangular spot that marks where she was placed has started to grow, and if so, how much. Have they raked the leaves that have gathered there? What will it look like when the bronze marker I ordered gets installed?

I wonder what I will feel as I slowly walk to that spot and if I'll say anything about the emptiness when I get there. What will my emotions do? Is it okay to say out loud what's in my heart? Will it seem weird to speak to someone who can't hear me? Is it right to continue telling her how much I love and miss her? I never worry about crying because that always happens. I can't not cry. Do I share what's been going on since she died?

Today, as I pulled into the cemetery entrance, a song came on the radio. It was Roy Orbison singing "Pretty Woman." It wrecked me. It demolished me. For years, I wanted to sing it to her while kneeling in front of her and looking up into her happy and welcoming eyes. I never did it because, sadly, I was always waiting for the perfect moment to do it. It hit hard today when I realized how many of those perfect moments I must have missed in the forty-six years we shared life. I realized that any moment I sang it to her would have been perfect. Today, I talked to a pretty woman in her plot and shared my sadness over missing the moment.

The visit—I know by now that each one will be as different as it is special.

It's a Matter of Form.

It's just about six months since she died. Not one minute has replicated any of the time before her passing. This is a journey where the central theme doesn't change. It's that thing called grief. I'm discovering that it continues to come in different forms. Grieving because of the death of a close loved one doesn't stop. It has become synchronized with other additional reasons for grieving. Grief isn't the same; it's just a matter of form. Each of the further reasons for grieving arises *because* each is an outgrowth of the original grief I experienced with her passing.

It has taken me a while to recognize my feelings as grief arising from some of the other changes that have occurred. None of the changes are bad, per se, because they arose out of necessity and logical need. I was trying to look at each of the subsequent changes pragmatically. I was trying to force myself to think that because they were so logical and necessary, the worst thing that could happen is that I *might* experience a bit of melancholy.

Many months before Penny passed, I had started entertaining thoughts of retiring. Yes, at eighty and with sixty-six years of work under my belt, I thought it was time to hang it up. What scared me and helped me to procrastinate in retiring was the thought that I didn't know how not to work and that the unknown played heavily on my mind. My body had been barking at me for quite some time, and it was tired and a bit worn out. My wish-I-was forty-five-year-old mind said otherwise. So, five months after her passing, my body won the argument that it was time to retire and that I did. It took a while to recognize that I had opened myself up to more grief by doing so and that it wasn't simply a feeling of melancholy. My conscious focus had been the grief I carried from Penny's death. When I started to act a bit weird (my thought), someone pointed out that I had added a couple of

IT'S A MATTER OF FORM.

layers of grief on top of what I was already experiencing. I was grieving the closing of a monumental chapter—my work life. I was also experiencing the loss of a once robust body that allowed me to have that work-life all those years. My inner response to each was, "I'm done," and this is not how I thought it would end.

There was more grief waiting in the wings that I didn't anticipate. Again, I think that was because I was so aware of my grief over Penny that I was trying to deny that there could be any more grief to experience. This involved selling the house and moving into a fifty-five and older condominium building. When the process started, there were many things to do and think about, and it was relatively fast-paced. Even with the excitement of a quick sale, it suddenly hit me that I was parting ways with another considerable part of my story. We had lived in the "Old Girl" for forty-six years. We raised five kids into adulthood there. We, Grandpa and Grandma, raised a bunch of grandkids there. The home was a veritable memory factory. But the issue now was that it was merely a house and no longer a home. My heart ached to move out because of that, but it was also evident that I could no longer properly keep up with or care for the "Old Girl" as was needed. The realization that yet another chapter was ending produced a form of grief I had not experienced and added it to the grief pile I was experiencing.

Each event flew in the face of one of the cardinal "rules" for those grieving: Don't make any significant changes for a year. In my case, I felt, and still do, that the changes were necessary. I couldn't see, and still don't, how delaying those decisions would bear any good fruit. I felt that not making the changes would serve only bad fruit.

I mentioned above that I felt I was starting to act weird. I would cry (and try to hide it) at the craziest times. I felt like I couldn't shake this dark cloud that I sensed was over me: the melancholy cloud. At one point, I was sitting at the gate of an airport terminal. I sat there long because I got there well before my flight time. It didn't take long for me to start bawling for no apparent reason. I bawled during the flight and into the terminal where I had arrived. I could mentally find no trigger(s) for the continuing outburst. It was almost as if, "Well, I just want to cry." But I didn't want to, and yet I couldn't stop.

I believe, looking back at that and similar situations, that I was experiencing denied grief, grief in other forms. This grief wasn't just from the loss of anyone but rather the loss of several things. While it didn't have the deep sense of pain attached to it because of Penny's death, it nonetheless was unpleasant and unwanted grief. And it was hard to accept it as grief and embrace it as such.

Only God knows what lies ahead, and I must trust He knows what is best for me and when. He must be my rock as I continue to tread these unfamiliar waters.

> *"You can, for just a moment, fuse grief like a bone, but the memory of the ability to bend lingers inside, like an itch running in the blood, just beneath the skin: relief is always only temporary. Grief, we understood, would now hijack a part of our day for the rest of our lives, sneaking in, making the world momentarily stop, every day, forever."*
>
> ~ Emily Rapp~[16]

Perhaps the Worst First

I have dreaded quite a few things in my life, but none have had the emotional impact that approaching the first anniversary of her death has had on me. Much of the time, it seems as if she died just yesterday. I am glad about that freshness because I think it means that I still appreciate her influence and impact on my life—the things I smile fondly about as those memories arise.

Yet, the passage of time is difficult to embrace because it represents an emptiness I don't want. It's a stark reminder of the touches, hugs, kisses, and looks I no longer receive or can give. It's a harsh reminder that there is no longer a love language to engage in, tender words to share, goofy inside jokes to guffaw at, or even something said in anger that is ultimately forgiven. The looming first anniversary yells that all of that is over.

With the arrival of the first anniversary, a few unexpected changes have also come. Most notable of those has been the family dynamic. It's not the same; over time, I'm convinced it never will be. I'm sad about that. It's been shared with me that what I am experiencing is the rule rather than the exception and that it is probably typical for a widower, especially in a blended family such as we had. The relationship with most of the kids is different now. Mom, the rock, the glue that held it all together, is gone. The "check-ins" by phone or visits by the kids that were so prevalent over the past thirty to thirty-five years don't happen anymore. The silence is loud. I have found myself at times trying to put myself on a guilt trip about the matter by wondering, "What did I do wrong?" or going through a whole slew of "I shoulds" or "what ifs." I have once again found relief from the wisdom of others. I am now okay to accept that it is all about choices and that I cannot control which choices others make. And I can (and should) love them through their choices regardless of how I feel about those choices.

Finally, when I last saw her lying in her casket at the funeral home before we went to the cemetery, the kids asked me about the wedding rings still on her finger. I told them that the rings were where they belonged, that they were a part of her, an essential part of our journey together, one that wouldn't end with her passing. That was as important to me then as it is now. My left ring finger still carries that band of gold she gave me when we were married, and it still holds the same weight in my heart as it did that day, perhaps even more so now. It's a badge that I am proud of. It represents what she meant to me and her role in my life. It's also an honor I can bestow on her, even though she is not here. She was my life then, and nothing about that has changed except for her physical presence—a presence that this, the first anniversary, defines differently and with different emotions.

> *"The reality is that you will grieve forever. You will not 'get over' the loss of a loved one; you'll learn to live with it. You will heal and you will rebuild yourself around the loss you have suffered. You will be whole again, but you will never be the same. Nor should you be the same nor would you want to."*
> ~Elisabeth Kübler-Ross~[17]

Prologue

```
            through you.

    i tried to run away from grief.
    it followed me.
    i tried to bandage it up.
    it split wide open.
    i tried to push it down into my chest.
    my heart began to burst.
    i tried to hide it in a smile.
    my tears still found a way.
    i tried to bury it in the ground.
    it sprouted and grew even bigger.
    i kept myself busy.
    it reached in and said,
    "i'm not done with you yet."
    grief cannot be walked around.
    it must come through you.

                ullie-kaye
```

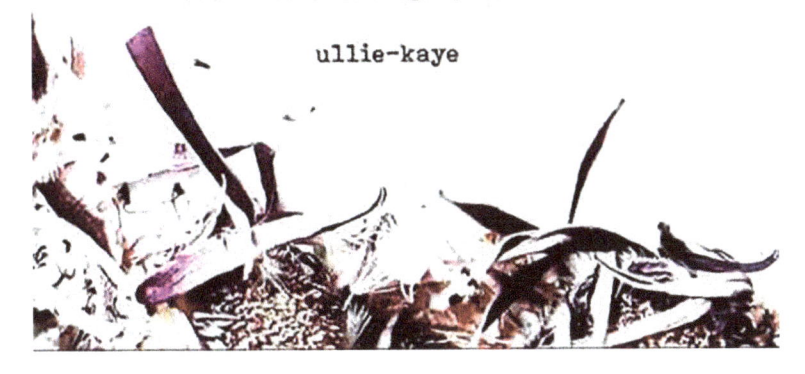

This book will never have an ending until I pass away. It will end at that time because that's when my grief journey will end.

There are some things about grief that I now know. I know that I could never fully understand the grief anyone felt over the passing of a loved one until death visited my doorstep. I know that grief will be a permanent part of my life moving forward. I know that life as I knew it has changed, and it will change more. I know my faith in God helped pull me through the most terrible time of my life, and it will continue to do so. I know there will be times when I will wrestle with God, and there will be moments when I will likely be angry at Him. I know that He will never turn His back on me because of it, and I know that she is resting in His arms, waiting for me, and though she is gone, her love is still nestled in my heart.

Rest in peace, babe . . . I'll see you later.

Ending Comments

Earlier in the book, I talked about the veritable flood and the fact that the flood included people who not only walked alongside me in this grief journey but, in some instances, carried me. I could not have made that journey alone. My head was too rattled, and my heart was too broken. Most of those wonderful souls still help me carry the water even today.

Greg and Connie Bowman have unfailingly shared their hearts, wisdom, and love with me. They have poured themselves into me, and I am deeply grateful for the peace and calm their presence brings to my life. On their shirttails are my Westridge Community Church family, who continue to support me.

Don Walker, who has led a Grief Ministry for several years, freely gives his time to hear me out when I'm at my worst as he mentors me in this journey I don't want to be on.

Ullie-Kaye, of Ullie-Kaye Poetry (Author of Fires), unknowingly calmed my soul through the words she so often posted on social media before she published her book.

Michelle Bollom, Linda Drachenberg Mueller, Jennifer Massie Cabernoch, and Gretchen Miller Carolan, each of whom belongs to the Joe Miller Big Mouth Cheerleader Squad, always and without fail checked in and offered encouragement when I was writing this book.

The staff at my publisher, Xulon Press, were outstanding in their answers to my many questions while writing this book. They were patient when I asked stupid questions as they walked me through the answers.

I am sure I missed some folks who made up the flood, and I apologize for that. Life is all about relationships and a sense of community, especially

ENDING COMMENTS

during adversity or challenges. Leaning into others is so important during those times, as I discovered during my adversity.

Thank you all, and God Bless you.

About the Author

Joe Miller, known online as @oldguywritesbooks, resides in Illinois and is the father of seven grown children. A widower, he spends his extra time working on his writing career. He plays a pivotal role in community ministry at his church and serves as a leader and mentor with Men at the Cross, a prominent men's ministry organization. Joe's diverse background includes a career as a police officer and ownership of several businesses before retirement. His spiritual discovery and personal growth journey inspired him to share his insights through writing. Joe is a published songwriter and author. His books reflect his passion for grace, hope, and transformative change. His writings resonate with readers seeking deeper meaning and renewal in their lives.

Further Reading

Miller, Joe, *A Better Man, Husband, Father*, Maitland, FL, Xulon Press, 2015

It is a book full of snippets of everyday things (situations, thoughts, actions, relational matters) that can lead a man to make transformative choices.

Lamott, Anne, *Bird by Bird*, New York, NY, Anchor Books, 2019

This is a book chock full of lively, big-hearted, homespun advice and simple words of wisdom about life and writing.

Bell, Steve & Valerie, *Coming Back*, Wheaton, IL, Victor Books, 1993

Grief significantly threatens the spiritual grounding of most people experiencing it. It's easy to cry, "Where is God in all this?" *Coming Back* is a collection of poignant and heart-rending stories about real-life cases of spiritual survivorship.

Miller, Joe, *Dog Walk Talk; While I'm Walking, God's Talking*, Maitland, FL, Xulon Press, 2020

In *Dog Walk Talk . . .*, Joe has written a hope-filled and encouraging book that focuses on the questions many ask, "Why do I do what I do?" and "Why don't I do that which I ought to do?"

Ullie-Kaye, *Fires—Hardship, Grief, and Perseverance*, Monee, IL, KDP Publishing, 2024

Fires is a collection of poems by Canadian author Ullie-Kaye. The reader is invited to journey along in whatever capacity they have experienced hardship, grief, and perseverance.

Miller, Joe, *God Said It. Not Me*, Maitland, FL, Xulon Press, 2024

This is a book through which the author shares a different God. God is not some old ogre who's just "out there somewhere." He is real and contemporary, as the author shares how he thinks God would respond directly to our hearts as we face different life situations today.

Resource Page

Image 1: https://abutterfly.beauty/losing-a-loved-one-to-cancer-quotes

Image 2: https://www.lovetoknow.com/life/grief-loss/losing-someone-cancer-quotes-strength-comfort

Image 3: https://www.andersenpress.co.uk/factory-and-andersen-press-to-partner-on-new-animated-series-of-david-mckees-elmer-the-patchwork-elephant/

Image 4: https://www.pexels.com/photo/abstract-art-adobe-photoshop-art-art-exhibition-1170822/

Image 5: https://www.pexels.com/photo/blurred-portrait-of-a-man-10877499/

Image 6: https://www.pexels.com/photo/man-in-yellow-crew-neck-t-shirt-pointing-a-finger-4584538/

Image 7: https://quotefancy.com/quote/47903/Esther-Earl-Isn-t-it-sad-that-so-often-it-takes-facing-death-to-appreciate-life-and-each

Image 8: https://futureofworking.com/101-short-condolence-messages-for-loss-of-a-mother/

Image 9: https://www.pexels.com/photo/crystal-stream-flowing-thorough-grassy-glade-5118378/

Image 10: https://www.pexels.com/photo/medical-stethoscope-with-red-paper-heart-on-white-surface-4386467/

Image 11: https://www.pexels.com/photo/couple-lying-down-and-taking-selfie-7911314/

Image 12: https://www.pexels.com/photo/flooded-road-and-a-warning-sign-17752086/

Image 13: https://www.pexels.com/photo/senior-man-covering-mouth-with-hands-7544701/

Image 14: https://www.pexels.com/photo/a-person-doing-a-thumbs-up-9486674/

Image 15: https://www.pexels.com/photo/yes-written-in-the-sand-4711021/

Image 16: https://www.pexels.com/photo/selective-focus-photography-of-meat-on-grill-2491273/

Image 17: photograph by author

image 18: photograph by author

Images 19-38: photographs by author

Image 39: https://www.pexels.com/photo/silhouette-of-a-person-standing-on-a-rock-3283907/

Image 40: https://www.pexels.com/photo/grassy-meadow-with-flowers-in-nature-6858608/

Image 41: https://www.pexels.com/photo/close-up-photography-of-white-horse-2600383/

Image 42: https://www.pexels.com/photo/empty-white-photo-frames-on-wooden-surface-7319333/

RESOURCE PAGE

Image 43: https://www.pexels.com/photo/close-up-shot-of-a-rear-view-mirror-of-a-car-5268219/

Image 44: https://www.pexels.com/photo/stainless-faucet-861414/

Image 45: photograph by author

Image 46: https://www.pexels.com/photo/road-through-cemetery-in-summer-18493592/

Image 47: photograph by author

Image 48: https://www.pexels.com/photo/book-page-2228578/

Image 49: Used with the permission of ullie-kaye, author, Fires, Self-Published, Monee, IL, Aug. 8, 2024, page 134.

Image 50: photograph by author

Endnotes

1. Jose N. Harris, Mi Vida, 2010, Bloomington, IN, Xlibris, 436

2. Pink Floyd, 1979 Columbia Records side A, 1980

3. Jim Beaver, Life's That Way, 2009, New York, NY, Putnam Adult, 303

4. Matt Haig, Reasons to Stay Alive, 2016, Westminster London, Penguin Life, 256

5. Narrator Jeremy Childs, Thomas Nelson Publishers, 2012

6. Mirriam-Webster Dictionary, 2022, Springfield, MA, 960

7. Nancy Leigh Demass, The Quiet Place, 2012, Chicago, IL, Moody Publishers, 400

8. Mirriam-Webster Dictionary, 2022, Springfield, MA, 960

9. "I'll Say Yes." Track 8 on I'll Say Yes. Brooklyn Tabernacle Choir. 2017

10. Sherrilyn Kenyon, Acheron, 2008, New York, NY, St. Martin's Press, 723

11. Mitch Albom, For One More Day, 2006, Westport, CN, Hyperion, 208

12. Anne Lamott, Bird by Bird, 1995, Palatine, IL, Anchor Press, 238

13. Helen Keller, The Story of My Life, 1990, New York, NY, Bantam Classics, 240

14. Richard Paul Evans, The Sunflower, 2005, New York, NY, Simon & Schuster, 352

15. Melina Marchetta, On the Jellico Road, 2006, Camberwell, Victoria, AU, Penguin Australia, 290

ENDNOTES

[16] Emily Rapp, The Still Point of the Turning World, 2013, New York, NY, Penguin Press HC, 272

[17] Elisabeth Kubler-Ross, On Grief and Grieving, 2007, New York, NY, Scribner, 256